We all have a network...the question is whether it is the right network for you? Janine is an expert at helping people identify who their network is—do you have the right people at the right stage in your career and life to help guide, steer, cheer and challenge you on your journey? Networking is not about collecting business cards or LinkedIn connections but about strategically identifying and engaging with the selected individuals who form your tribe to help you achieve your goals. *It's Who You Know* will show you how.

Julia Van Graas, Partner EY

Finally—a fresh alternative to networking that makes sense. This is a book for smart people on a quest to build quality connections.

**Dr Jason Fox, best-selling author of The Game Changer *and*
How to Lead a Quest**

Janine Garner is a true connector of people and has helped teach, support and encourage countless women and men from the corporate industry and private business owners to drive deeper, stronger results through her excellent business acumen and experience. *It's Who You Know* is absolutely essential reading for those who wish to learn the best personal networking strategies or for those who are at a stage where they wish to re-energise their professional and personal goals and kick-start the process to achieve more!

Olivia Walsh, Head of Talent Development and Diversity APAC, CBRE

Build a strategic network before you change the world. Leaders know that it's not just what you know, it's also who you know that defines 21st century success. We may be the sum total of the five people we know and spend time with. This book shows you how to be strategic and intentional about how you do that. Janine embodies thi̵ ̵ ̵ ̵ ̵ ̵ l is the perfect thought leader on the topic.

**Matt Church, best-selling author ̵ ̵ ̵ ̵ ̵ ̵ ̵ ̵ ̵ ̵ ̵ ̵ ̵man
of Thought Leaders Global**

I'm a real-world example that wl ̵ ̵ ̵ ̵ ̵ ̵ ̵ ̵ ̵ ̵ok works. I have worked closely with her ovei ̵ ̵ ̵ ̵ ̵ ̵ of years expanding the influence of the top talent in n ̵ ̵ ̵ ̵ ̵ ̵ ̵sation. Janine has brought many individuals from her personal network to the table to share their experiences. You have to make your network matter, and it's a two-way street. You have to read this book.

Duncan Smith, VP, Hewlett Packard Enterprise

Networking genius. Whether you hate networking or love it, this book is a must read. It will change the way you network forever. Janine shows us how to network in a way that is easier, better, more fun and more effective. Exhale. Networking just got less awkward and more awesome.

Kieran Flanagan, CCO, The Impossible Institute

Running your own business can be lonely. I've learned that having a Nexus of 12 key people around me is crucial. There's the person that will give me a hug, the person that challenges my thinking and the one that promotes me, even when I don't feel like promoting myself. The most important thing about my network is the diversity (gender, age, cultural background, industry) — all bring a different perspective to my thinking. This is all thanks to Janine!

Kelly Slessor, CEO, BanterMob

It's Who You Know is a must read for anyone in business who wants to achieve and succeed. Packed with practical tools and sound advice, Janine smashes the old paradigm of networking and shows the reader the power of building a small and supportive network based on authentic relationships.

Gabrielle Dolan, best-selling author of Ignite *and* Stories for Work

Networking is often feared and more often misunderstood. The conventional concept of networking conjures up images of name badges, cheap plonk and contrived conversations—the stuff of nightmares! The approach Janine has created is a fundamental game changer. She provides a holistic framework that benefits both career and lifestyle. It truly provides a competitive advantage and not only benefits you but the tribe you create.

Cian Zoller, Hewlett Packard Enterprise

IT'S
WHO
YOU
KNOW

JANINE GARNER

IT'S
WHO
YOU
KNOW

HOW A NETWORK OF
(12) KEY PEOPLE
CAN FAST-TRACK YOUR SUCCESS

WILEY

First published in 2017 by John Wiley & Sons Australia, Ltd
42 McDougall St, Milton Qld 4064
Office also in Melbourne

Typeset in 11/13 pt BerkeleyStd Book

© Curious Minds Pty Ltd 2017

The moral rights of the author have been asserted

National Library of Australia Cataloguing-in-Publication data:

Creator:	Garner, Janine, author.
Title:	It's Who You Know: how a network of 12 key people can fast-track your success / Janine Garner.
ISBN:	9780730336846 (pbk.)
	9780730336860 (ebook)
Notes:	Includes index.
Subjects:	Career development.
	Strategic planning.
	Success in business.
	Business networks.
	Interpersonal relations.

Cover design by Wiley

Cover images © tai11/Shutterstock

Figures by Presentation Studio

Printed in Singapore by C.O.S. Printers Pte Ltd

10 9 8 7 6 5 4 3 2 1

Disclaimer
The material in this publication is of the nature of general comment only, and does not represent professional advice. It is not intended to provide specific guidance for particular circumstances and it should not be relied on as the basis for any decision to take action or not take action on any matter which it covers. Readers should obtain professional advice where appropriate, before making any such decision. To the maximum extent permitted by law, the author and publisher disclaim all responsibility and liability to any person, arising directly or indirectly from any person taking or not taking action based on the information in this publication.

CONTENTS

About the author	ix
Acknowledgements	xi
Foreword by Lisa Messenger	xiii
Assess your network online	xvii
Introduction	xix

PART I: WHY — **1**

1: SHIFT your mindset — 3
2: RETHINK how you network now — 13
3: TRANSFORM to a collective network — 27

PART II: WHO — **39**

4: SORT through your current network — 41
5: SEARCH for your Core Four — 53
6: SEEK out your 12 key people and personalities — 71
7: SINK the 12 Shadow Archetypes — 101

PART III: HOW — **115**

8: CHOOSE who, what and why — 117
9: CONNECT in the right way — 131
10: CULTIVATE connections and exchange value — 143

Final words — 161
One last checklist — 163
Notes — 171
Index — 173
Let's connect — 181

ABOUT THE AUTHOR

Janine Garner loves connecting and collaborating with people, bringing them together to do incredible things. This is the heart and soul of everything she does both personally and professionally.

Janine delivers keynotes to corporates on the power of open and transparent relationships, mentors and motivates leaders and entrepreneurs, and facilitates workshops on building connected networks that accelerate success — all while managing a family of three young children with her husband.

Janine understands how hard but important it is to build a strategic and smart network that can support you through the good times and the bad. More than once she has packed up her life in a suitcase, leaving behind a corporate career, learning from business start-ups and failures to start afresh.

Originally from Yorkshire in the UK, she worked her way across the world, putting together award-winning marketing campaigns and strategies for high-profile brands such as Ralph Lauren, Oroton, Jaeger, Sainsbury's Homebase and Citizen Watches.

Janine is a partner at Thought Leaders Global, which helps clever people to become commercially smart, and is founder and CEO of the LBDGroup, a networking community that connects like-minded women to help them achieve extraordinary growth.

Her client list models the perfect diverse network. She works with men and women from all walks of life, from a wide range of industries and with varied experience across the globe, including IT execs, lawyers, retail operators, fitness gurus and multinational CEOs, as well as companies such as Hewlett Packard Enterprise,

CBRE, EY, Clayton UTZ, Servcorp, Fernwood Fitness, Bras N Things, Scentre Group, ANZIIF and APSMA, to name a few.

Janine was awarded an Honorary Doctorate of Science in 2016, and holds a Bachelor of Science in Management and Business Administration. She has won an International Stevie Award, has been a top 10 finalist in the *DARE Magazine* Daredevil Awards and has been listed as one of Australia's 'Most Inspiring Women' by *Madison Magazine*.

Her first book, *From Me to We: Why commercial collaboration will future-proof business, leaders and personal success*, was published by Wiley in 2014.

She is often on TV or radio, and her inspirational words and insights are regularly published in the media by *The Huffington Post*, *CEO Magazine*, *Success Magazine*, *BRW*, *Women's Agenda*, *AIM* and *The Australian*.

Janine believes that by networking we create opportunities to mutually exchange value, that this transforms our connections and our lives, and that only we ourselves have the power to bring about this transformation. Her life is proof that success is not so much about what you know as about *who* you know.

janinegarner.com.au

ACKNOWLEDGEMENTS

This book would not have been possible without my own network of Promoters, Pit Crew, Teachers and Butt-kickers—the many friends, family, colleagues and clients who collaborated on developing my thinking, allowed me to question and delve into their networking behaviour and who ultimately encouraged me to keep going. A sincere thank you to each of you, I couldn't have written this book without you all.

A huge thank you to the extraordinary team and talent around me who helped extract this book from my head to paper. Thank you to my incredible editor, Kelly Irving. Your passion for this project and your compassion and smarts throughout those long days, late nights and many weekends—quite simply wow—I will be forever grateful. To the extraordinary team at Presentation Studio, and in particular Emma Bannister and Sarah Marriot, thank you for all your design genius and for turning my crappy sketches into something far superior. And of course to the team at Wiley for your dedication and support—Lucy Raymond, Chris Shorten, Jem Bates, Ingrid Bond and Theo Vassili—thank you.

To my incredible team who have supported me from the sidelines—Lisa Dunne thank you for keeping on top of everything, for looking after all our fabulous clients and always exploring ways to go one step beyond—it doesn't go unnoticed. To Lee Ussher, Melissa Browne and Scott Eathorne thank you for everything, for thinking big with me, for listening to my endless conversations, for strategising with me, for adding to my thinking and for keeping me true and on track.

A huge thank you to those that challenged me to write this book—my colleagues and fellow thought leaders that inspire me with every conversation to think more and to be more. Matt Church, I will be forever grateful for your guidance and mentorship from the beginning and it is now an honour to partner alongside you and the team at Thought Leaders. To Lynne Cazaly, Pete Cook, Dr Jason Fox, Dan Gregory, Gabrielle Dolan, Christina Guidotti thank you for being the individuals that you are, for all the conversations and the continuing encouragement. Thank you, Kieran Flanagan for working through the Nexus with me as we crafted the descriptions, for your weekly check-ins, for always finding a way to put my frustrations into perspective and for making me laugh too many times — don't stop! I am so grateful to you all for your support and friendship.

To Lisa Messenger — you are an inspiration to me and so many others. Thank you for your continuous support and your encouragement to think big and push to challenge the status quo always. You were there at the beginning of this journey as I transitioned from my corporate role and I am grateful for your support right here, right now. Thank you for taking the time to pen the foreword for this book — you epitomise all that exists when we network the right way.

And finally an enormous shout out to my own little tribe of amazingness. Jason, thank you for your ongoing support—always. Without you none of this would have been possible. Thank you for always believing and pushing me to follow my dreams and to become more, for creating the space for me to think and for keeping on top of everything while I bunkered down to write this book. To my gorgeous and amazing children—Flynn, Taya and Carter—you all continue to amaze me with all you are doing and all you are becoming. Keep dreaming big because the world quite simply is your oyster and you are all part of the change the world needs. Thank you for your patience and understanding, for the endless sneaky chocolate biscuits, and for surprising Mummy with her very own superpowered wonder woman. My life is more amazing having you all in it.

And to you, the reader. Thank you for taking the time to read this book; to be open to a new way of doing things. Curiosity creates opportunity and my wish for you is that this book opens up a whole new world of opportunity to take control of your own success.

FOREWORD BY LISA MESSENGER

Over a decade ago, I helped a budding entrepreneur and motivational speaker with his PR strategy. To me, that component of business was incredibly simple, second nature, the sort of stuff I could do in my sleep, but to him it was a juggernaut, a mystery, a pot of gold at the end of the rainbow he craved and undeniably needed for the systematic growth of his business and personal brand.

So there we were, a flat white for him and an iced mocha for me, sunshine on our backs, pens and paper everywhere. I talked him through the media landscape philosophically and practically; we discussed his approach, the concept of bespoke pitching, potential roadblocks, long-term strategy versus quick wins, and then I did something simple but oh so valuable: I introduced him to some of my own contacts.

A couple of months later, I saw a feature about him pop up in a national newspaper. Then again four months later, but this time he was being announced as a regular contributor to a national publication. He was later featured on some pretty heavy-hitting international websites and then came the publication of his book.

I have watched from the sidelines over the years as his business profile has grown, and each time I spot him in the media or see his name listed as an event speaker, a small smile of pride grows on my face. Top line, I'm thrilled for him and hope it gets bigger and grander, whatever his personal vision might be. But on a personal level of reflection for me, I'm grateful to have played a part in someone else's success, realising that when you connect the right people together through a positive exchange, their success is also yours. After all, I played a part in his little wins, which have grown into big ones, and it all started with a handful of mutual introductions.

There is enormous value in making connections with the right people at the right time and with the right message or request. It is something I have always been passionate about and have focused on at every stage of my business life, believing deeply in the values of generosity and reciprocity. The people we connect with can make or break our ideas and future success. And we can do the same for them.

Making headway in business (or life) can be darned hard work. There can be roadblocks at every turn, or just a few roadblocks you simply can't seem to overcome. And one of the biggest mistakes you can make is going it alone when other people can often be the key.

In a few short years, I'm very happy to say, Collective Hub has grown into a global movement: the print magazine is sold in almost 40 countries (and always expanding); our online community unites hundreds of thousands of people from all over the world; we run massive events, have global book deals and have even started our own education course. And you'd be right to wonder how we have achieved this.

The short answer is a *lot* of very hard work and a relentless pursuit of our goals. There is no denying that we kept going in a sea of 'nos' when others would have turned back or fallen over from sheer exhaustion, and for that I'm crazily proud of myself and my team. But there are also some silent celebrators in our success. For, sprinkled along the way, there have been some very key and rather kind people who have catapulted our accomplishments in certain areas. To a few — I hope very much they know who they are — I will be forever grateful. One helped me find the right book agent for my US deal, another connected me with our international distributor, a third provided the connection to some very key players of US media, two were the conduits to my connection with big global thinkers such as Richard Branson, and another suggested the exact consultant needed at a pivotal financial time in the business's journey. Then there have been people who simply connected me with a like-minded individual or connected Collective Hub with a like-minded organisation, and magic happened as a result. While it was definitely up to me, up to us, to *make* something of those connections, the seeds of success were sown at the point of connection.

Connection is powerful, essential and far-yielding, and this book has the tools to help you realise that, develop your network and leverage its potential. Don't be so arrogant as to think you don't need others or too afraid to play a big game with global game changers. Be genuine and consistent in your approach, intentional rather than organic and always, *always* reciprocate. This is your moment ... but perhaps the best place to start is to actually make it someone else's as well.

Lisa Messenger
Founder and editor-in-chief of Collective Hub
collectivehub.com

ASSESS YOUR NETWORK ONLINE

As you're about to learn, a small and strategic network is crucial to your success.

Throughout the book I refer to resources, checklists and worksheets you can use to help you assess and reassess your network. These resources can be downloaded from my website: **janinegarner.com.au/resources.**

You can also review your network by applying the online diagnostic tool I have designed specifically for use alongside this book (visit **janinegarner.com.au/nexus**). By unravelling what kind of network you have now and who among the 12 key people are currently missing from your network, this diagnostic will help you build a network that works best for you.

As you'll soon see, reviewing your network is not a one-off activity. You need to reassess your network at key points in your life and career to respond to new goals and different aspirations you have.

So use these resources while you're reading this book, then return to them again and again as your goals and aspirations change. This is the real secret to a successful, strategic network.

Build a network that works for you, share insights that matter to others. Connect. Collaborate. Succeed.

INTRODUCTION

Network – Connect – Collaborate – Succeed

How many times have you been told that 'you really have to network', that networking is 'essential for your growth and personal success'?

Do you jump up and down with joy at this idea, eager to get out there and meet new people? Or do you cringe with horror, thinking you'd much rather be spending your time doing something you actually enjoy or something that seems more productive than notching up a couple more friends on your Facebook page?

The truth is, the adage 'It's not what you know, it's who you know' has more weight now than ever.

Today 'busy' is a status update and everyone is your 'friend', so it's harder to make connections that really count, beyond adding to the number of followers on your Twitter account.

Job vacancies are filled before they are advertised and previously unthought-of collaborations appear out of nowhere to create new and competitive markets and steal market share. Add to this the constant pressure of coming up with new ideas to help us remain relevant and influential in a saturated business landscape and it's no wonder most of us hide behind our computers and feel paralysed with fear.

Sure, networking still matters, but your network matters more.

So who is in your network and how much input or influence do they have on what you're doing or trying to achieve? How well do they really, truly know you? How much can they help you?

There is no doubt that building a sales lead generation list is critical for the growth of many a business endeavour, and the explosion of social media has made finding particular networks easier, but has it made your network any *better*?

There is much more to networking than collecting likes, friends, connections or old-school business cards. To really succeed, and break out beyond the online realm, you must become the master of your network both at work and in life generally.

The right network is about having the right people and the right relationships in your professional and personal life.

Without any network at all, opportunities are missed, new possibilities aren't spotted, your thinking stagnates, and the dreams and career aspirations you once had become unreachable. You change jobs, move location — and suddenly you have to start out all over again. You find it hard to push through tough times, to get that job or promotion, to sell that idea, *to get noticed*.

Over the past couple of decades I've worked in the corporate and entrepreneurial space with people across geographical regions, functions and industries, people with a wide variety of backgrounds and experience. I've had the opportunity to interview master networkers such as Emergent CEO Holly Ransom and seven-time world surf champion Layne Beachley. I've studied leaders and entrepreneurs such as Richard Branson, Oprah Winfrey and Michael Bloomberg to figure out how they achieve their goals and what makes them tick. Who are the people they surround themselves with and how much do these choices influence their success?

Every one of the people I have worked with, spoken to or studied attests to the fact that true success lies in surrounding yourself with a small yet strong, trusted and tight network — a network that works with you and for you.

I spent the first 10 years of my corporate career in the UK. After leaving the relative safety of my protected Yorkshire childhood and graduating from Aston University, Birmingham, I moved to London to take up my first job, my new life packed in a bag and only my university friends for support. I learned very early on of the importance of a network both in life and at work. I experienced the impact of major company shake-ups, new CEOs forming new leadership teams that swiftly took over from former colleagues. Strategic direction, company values and day-to-day culture changed at what seemed like a whim. Nothing and no-one felt safe.

At the age of 29 I moved to Australia, once more with dreams of a new life packed in a bag, forced to build up another network of trusted colleagues, clients and friends. As I moved up the corporate ranks, I witnessed first-hand how seniority attracts more influence and means greater impact, how an elevated job title and a bigger budget can magically open doors and make things happen. Yet as connected as I was from a business point of view, without a true, authentic network to turn to I felt increasingly isolated.

In 2011, I struck out on my own, launching the LBDGroup, a niche community of like-minded, results-oriented businesswomen, female corporate leaders and entrepreneurs who connect, contribute and collaborate to drive commercial success for each other. Over the years, this network has come to represent so much more than generating business leads for ourselves and one another. The cross-functional, cross-industry nature of this collective stretches people's thinking, propels goals and plans, and creates more new opportunities at both a personal and professional level than would ever have been possible had we all gone it alone.

As the LBDGroup has grown in size, mini networks have evolved as individuals have created strategically appropriate networks for themselves within the broader network. I have built my own network of Promoters, Teachers, Pit Crew and Butt-kickers. They are the people who see more in me than I do myself, people who make me better, push me further and encourage me to do more. I have experienced the power of true connection, support and encouragement. Together we share learnings and insights, open doors for each other, push each other to go for it, to achieve more, because 'I know you can'. My personal network is small, it's tight, it's uber-connected and it's absolutely the pit crew of smarts that helps me achieve my goals.

This book is a culmination of all of my experience and insights. It challenges the status quo of what we've come to learn and believe about networking. You'll read real interviews and case studies, and find examples of real people (with some names changed for privacy) who have struggled with networking but have learned to make a small, strategic network work for them.

Here's the bottom line: It's about quality not quantity. We don't need more contacts, we don't need more 'friends' and we don't necessarily need to spend more time connecting online. If this was all we needed, then every one of us would be enjoying unparalleled success through the sheer number of opportunities we have to connect.

Leadership expert John C. Maxwell says,

> Those closest to you determine your level of success, so choosing the right companions as partners in pursuit of your vision is an important decision. My advice is to surround yourself with talented people who will challenge you, help you grow and inspire you to maximize your potential.

It's time to create a new plan of action — one that puts you in control, identifies the right people for you and creates the right behaviours that will nurture your network for mutual success.

Everyone needs a network, whether you are a recent graduate hunting for your first job, a manager who has just scored a promotion, a parent planning on running your first marathon, a philanthropist, leader, consultant, entrepreneur, speaker, freelancer or writer — it doesn't matter what you do, what level you operate on, what industry you are in and whether you work for an organisation or out on your own.

So this book is for you. It will encourage you to throw out society's expectations and what you feel you 'should' be doing, and instead start to think smart and strategically.

You'll review your network as it is now to determine:

- what you are doing that is and isn't working
- who is in your network now and who should be
- who is adding value and who is draining your energy
- how to leverage a key network—a Nexus—of only 12 key people and personalities.

You'll find the tools and skills you need to:

- take control of your network
- master the art of real and influential networking in a noisy and disconnected online world
- build a transformational network of 12 key people to fast-track your success
- leverage and use your skills to your advantage
- nurture and maintain these relationships on an ongoing basis.

As you read, you'll have plenty of opportunities to workshop your own personal situation through checklists, worksheets and other resources available in this book and online at my website (**janinegarner.com.au/resources**). You can also review your network using my online diagnostic tool (at **janinegarner.com .au/nexus**).

I encourage you to use these resources at every opportunity to reassess your own network and create new success, not just now but into the future as your circumstances change.

I wrote *It's Who You Know* because I believe we all need to get back in control by building a 'Network of Me' where we are smack bang in the centre of critical connections with real influence and real impact, connections capable of transforming our thinking, challenging our behaviours and working collectively to build our positioning, elevate our profile and push us to achieve more.

Once you have read this book you will face a choice. Either take control of the people you surround yourself with and *own* your future, or stay out of control and allow your network to morph and shift depending on what is going on around you.

Former US president Franklin Delano Roosevelt once said, 'I'm not the smartest fellow in the world, but I can sure pick smart colleagues.'

Get in control of your network and you will change your game, make the impossible possible and achieve your goals. You will find it easier to connect to people with ideas and dreams and to convert those ideas and dreams into action.

So what do you say? Are you ready to build your own small, smart, supercharged network?

PART I
WHY

Networking is all about connecting, yet the way we're going about it now is all wrong! Most of our connections are superficial and transactional, and this will get us nowhere in our personal or professional life.

Many of us hate networking but recognise it as an essential skill if we want to get anywhere in life. You would not have picked up this book in the first place if you thought otherwise! No matter what you do, where you work or what industry you're in, your network is a crucial tool for professional and personal growth.

So what is the right way to network? More importantly, what is the *wrong* way to network, and how do you avoid that?

What matters most is to invest the time, energy and commitment into strategically building a small but smart network for you. Connecting with a group of people who work with you, alongside you, ahead of you and behind you will help ensure you have the right information and make the right decisions at the right time. Without doubt, this will fast-track your future. I'm so confident about this that I hereby invite you to contact me and call me out if it does not!

Part I introduces some of the essentials of networking.

There are three key stages to understanding networking and reassessing how you think and approach your network:

1. SHIFT. What's the deal with networking now? Why are we so over it? Chapter 1 will explore why it's so important to shift our thinking on networking.

2. RETHINK. What's the right way to network? What's the wrong way? We'll look at the differences in chapter 2.

3. TRANSFORM. How do we build a network that works? Why is the power in the people? Chapter 3 answers this question.

Now let's get started.

Shift your mindset

The 2012 movie *Disconnect* features three different groups of characters, their search for connection and their dependence on technology. A young married couple who recently lost a baby have their identities stolen and exposed online. Two teenagers use Facebook to cyber-bully a lonely and unpopular classmate whose hardworking lawyer father is so hardwired to his phone that he can't find the time to communicate with his family. An ambitious TV reporter uncovers a story about an 18-year-old webcam porn performer that could make her career—then she falls in love with him.

These disparate stories become increasingly entangled and connected as the film progresses. By the end (spoiler alert!), they all come to realise that what is most important in life is the love they share with those closest to them, from whom they have become estranged and disconnected.

Connecting. Networking. Sounds simple, maybe too simple. These are not new concepts. Rather, connecting and networking have been the cornerstones of good business since business began.

As explored in the movie *Disconnect*, the internet has opened up a whole new world of content, connections and networking possibilities. The explosion of digital and social media has fundamentally changed the way we function, communicate and do business both online and offline.

Yet the technology that was supposed to connect us and bring us closer together actually seems to be having the reverse effect.

Something about how we are networking right now just isn't working.

When I first started networking back in the eighties, 22 years old and fresh out of university, the hardest part was knowing where to go for help and support. In those early days of my career, networking was mostly about hanging out with your crew from work at a nearby bar. If you were lucky enough to be invited to a company or industry function, you'd pull on your power suit of confidence and off you'd go armed with a wallet full of business cards and a 30-second elevator pitch.

The goal was to swap cards and chat with as many people as possible. This was relatively easy, albeit a little nerve-racking, though the cheap wine helped. The follow-up involved a phone call, or maybe a handwritten 'nice to meet you' note sent by snail mail, with the business card you'd just collected filed in your plump Rolodex or a plastic sleeve in a Filofax.

These days we are bombarded by multiple networking groups, industry-specific events and meet-ups through friends and colleagues or via LinkedIn, Facebook, Twitter and assorted other channels. Then there's speed networking (designed along the lines of speed dating), an event format in which you have a brief set time span to strike up a 'connection' before you have to move on to the next person.

But are we really connecting here?

#Connecting or #disconnecting?

American psychiatrist Edward Hallowell writes,

> Never in human history have our brains had to work with so much information as they do today ... We have a generation of

people who are so busy processing the information received from all directions that they are losing the ability to think and feel.

The explosion of social media has turned the world of face-to-face interactions upside down, opening up previously unimagined opportunities and ways of connecting with our friends, peers, existing and future clients, and complete strangers worldwide — all at the touch of a button. We are more connected than ever before through our smartphone, the internet, instant messaging and social media.

According to statsita.com, 'The power of social networking is such that the number of worldwide users is expected to reach some 2.95 billion by 2020, around a third of the Earth's entire population.' New social networking sites are popping up every minute. LinkedIn is growing at the rate of two new members per second.

With the increase in 'connection', however, has come a parallel increase in 'disconnection'.

In her book *Alone Together*, social psychologist Sherry Turkle argues that our relentless connection to the digital world is actually driving isolation. On the whole, she says, we are now 'more lonely and distant from one another ... This is not only changing the way we interact online, it's straining our personal relationships, as well.'

A 2013 study by Hanna Krasnova and a group of researchers from two German universities[1] examined the impact of envy on Facebook. The study concluded that one in three people felt worse after visiting Facebook. 'Lurkers' who spent time looking at everyone else's content, while not posting any of their own, felt especially dissatisfied. This behaviour led to feelings of loneliness, frustration and anger.

These feelings are encapsulated in the label FOMO, or Fear of Missing Out, which is defined in the Oxford Dictionary as 'anxiety that an exciting or interesting event may currently be happening elsewhere, often aroused by posts seen on social media'.

Social media encourages one-way communication. Status updates and shout-outs, overloading and oversharing of personal information and hashtags — #kidspam, #foodenvy, #bestdayever, #grateful, #inspired — make us look 'good' but feel 'bad', and add very little of actual value to our lives.

In reality, our actual conversations tend to be brief, fleeting and superficial. A quick scan of any café, restaurant, bus, train or footpath will suggest we're more interested in what is happening on our screens than in the people next to us — even our children, who are now babysat with Peppa Pig on the iPad.

Sure, we're connected, but increasingly to the digital world rather than to the real world and each other. Networking, on the other hand, relies on two-way communication: the mutual exchange of information and value.

So if we're feeling stressed out with all this frivolous one-way online communication, how has this affected the way we view and do networking?

The 'work' in network

So many of us avoid networking because we see it as exactly that — hard work. We've put the work back into networking and made it all too difficult and exhausting. The problem is that often the events we choose to attend have little relevance or value for us. For most of us, when we do network, we network within the narrow orbit of our immediate circle, tapping into like-minded circles of sympathetic people. This is fine as far as it goes, but it has limitations over time. By minimising difference of opinion and experience, it breeds laziness, stifles growth and limits potential.

Having spoken and worked with many people over the years I have studied the subject, I have found there are four key pain points we report feeling when it comes to networking. These are:

1. overwhelmed

2. overcomplicated

3. overstretched

4. over it!

Let's look at each of these in more detail.

1. Overwhelmed

Where do we begin? With all the online and offline options available to us, many of us feel overwhelmed by choice, with no idea where to start when it comes to building a network. Face-to-face engagement puts pressure on us to be constantly interesting and engaging; computers remove much of that pressure, so it's no wonder people opt to hide behind their smartphones and their like buttons. But how do we talk about ourselves or ask for help? And why would anyone care?

2. Overcomplicated

Which tools and applications should I use? Which social media networks should I be on — and should I join all, one or just some of them? How do I manage them? Given time constraints, how do I keep in touch with an ever-growing network? Which face-to-face events should I attend? How often do I need to 'network'?

These are just some of the many questions you face when it comes to the Rubik's cube of networking sites, events and groups.

Add to this the pressures of multitasking, having to think on your feet, constantly switching focus, jumping from one group of people to the next while trying to remember what actions you should take … Are you confused yet?

3. Overstretched

We struggle with prioritising the tasks on our to-do list, let alone deciding on who to call or get a cuppa with, or which networking event to attend. The follow-up conversations are often rushed and superficial, falling back on small talk and an obsessive fixation on the weather (or that could be the English in me). Words and messages are communicated through acronyms — LOL, FYI and OMG and the like, with more arcane expressions such as IRL, TBH and DFTBA (don't forget to be awesome) on the rise.

Every day we are pulled and stretched in hundreds of directions, challenged to be truly 'present' while maximising productivity despite the growing demands on our time and energy. Most of us report feeling drained, exhausted and overstretched much of the time. Throw networking into the mix, and many of us will say, 'I know I should, but I'll do it another day.'

4. Over it!

When it comes to networking, we are quite simply *over it*. We know we should network because everyone around us is telling us so, but where is the real evidence of the return? *Why should I network? Is it really necessary?* Most of us these days would rather be doing something else.

Why bother?

If we're feeling overwhelmed, confused, overstretched and over it, why on earth would we still bother networking?

It's simple really.

You can't get anywhere in life on your own.

Sheryl Sandberg, COO of Facebook, names Larry Summers, from the US Treasury Department and the World Bank, as her first and most important mentor. Fashion designer Yves St Laurent declares that Christian Dior 'taught me the basis of my art ... I never forgot the years I spent at his side'. Facebook gladiator Mark Zuckerberg learned about business and management practices from regular meetings with Apple founder Steve Jobs. Philanthropist and businessman Michael Bloomberg learned teamwork and ethics from William R. Saloman, managing partner of an investment bank where Bloomberg first worked.

A strong, connected and mutually beneficial network provides you with a series of stepping stones to success. The intentional support of another, with whom you collaborate and share what you know and who you know, pushes you forward in life.

The active and mutual support of others helps to:

- boost confidence
- achieve clear goals

- open doors to opportunity
- create business leads
- support decision making
- pave the path to success.

Countless articles and books have been written about the importance of networking. In his book *Highly Effective Networking*, Orville Pearson writes, 'When the economy is good networking is important. In tough times or tough job markets, networking is essential.'

It is imperative today to join forces with others, utilise your collective skills and experience, add new connections and insights, and communicate the support you need to step into your future. The beauty, as *Never Eat Alone* author Keith Ferrazzi puts it, is that 'by giving your time and expertise and sharing them freely, the pie gets bigger for everyone'.

One is a lonely number

It is widely assumed that entrepreneurs operate alone, overcoming all challenges and bringing their ideas to market out of sheer individual drive and personality. This could not be further from the truth! Entrepreneurs understand that it is essential to have a core network around them to maximise the chances of productive ideas coming to fruition.

Dame Anita Roddick, founder of cosmetics giant The Body Shop, once said: 'We entrepreneurs are loners, vagabonds, troublemakers. Success is simply a matter of finding and surrounding ourselves with those open-minded and clever souls who can take our insanity and put it to good use.'

Even Steve Jobs, who was widely recognised as a loner, is said to have shared with his biographer Walter Isaacson, 'Creativity comes from spontaneous meetings, from random discussions. You run into someone, you ask what they are doing, you say WOW and soon you're cooking up all sorts of ideas.'

A solid network of key players is like an invisible protective shield. It's often not the smartest person in the room who achieves success in life, but the one with the right networks and contacts.

Rita Pierson spent more than 40 years in and around the classroom. In her TED talk 'Every Kid Needs a Champion', she describes teaching classes that were so academically deficient it would reduce her to tears. One year she lied and told her students, 'You were chosen to be in my class because I am the best teacher and you are the best students, they put us together so we could show everybody else how to do it.' In a class test of 20 questions, one child got 18 questions wrong, so she gave him a +2 and a smiley face. When he asked if he had failed Rita responded, 'Yes... but you are on a roll, you got two right.'

This encouragement and support is exactly what gets you to where you want to go in life. And it simply cannot be done on your own.

Rework your network

Social media thought leader Mari Smith believes, 'Strategic, professional networking is one of the most powerful methods of growing your business in today's world.'

The key word here is *strategic*.

In 'Managing Yourself, A Smarter Way to Network' (*Harvard Business Review*, July 2011), Rob Cross and Robert J. Thomas found:

> The executives who consistently rank in the top 20% of their companies in both performance and well-being have diverse but select networks... made up of high-quality relationships with people who come from several different spheres and from up and down the corporate hierarchy.

We must build strategic connections around us, assembling a select group of people who open us to quality thinking and new perspectives.

Building a network that works is both an art and a science. It is an art in that it requires basic human skills in communication, connection, authenticity, and the ability to be 'in the present' and engaged with people and conversation.

It is a science in that building your network strategically requires an ongoing analysis and audit of your network, and a sustained curiosity around whether you're leveraging your network in the best way you can. It's about seeing the lines that connect people and ideas and create opportunity.

This means stripping away all the rubbish, reworking the way we network and connecting to others on a personal level with authenticity, meaning and value. It's time to start connecting with the right people in the right way, to learn how to build quality relationships.

You need to move from how many people you know to who are the right people to know.

Surround yourself with the right people, people who will guide and mentor you and cheer you on, people who will help shape the person you eventually become. It's up to you to choose your network wisely.

Take back control

Building a more valuable network means taking back ownership and control of your network and approaching your actions and connections with strategic deliberation.

When you align yourself with thinkers and doers who may have achieved what you dream of achieving or who simply ride shotgun alongside you, you'll be pushed to take the right actions and be inspired to move in the right direction towards your goals. This group of super-powers will build your success, boost your positive mojo and keep you in a place of constant growth.

Spend time with 'cup half empty' thinkers and you'll feel low and de-energised. Spend time with individuals who dream big and see the cup not just as half full but as overflowing, and you'll believe anything is possible.

You have to take ownership of your own network and to assess it continuously so it continues to evolve.

It's not about being in touch with as many people as possible; it's about finding the right people and the right relationships, as we'll explore in the next chapter.

If you want to fast-track your success, you need to take responsibility for your life, own the choices you make and spend time with those with a similarly positive attitude. Then you'll become a more proactive, positive individual with the ability to shape your own future.

Networking still a number one skill

Having a network has helped tremendously in shaping my career in multiple ways.

First, every career opportunity I have been given has come through my network. Second, my core network provides access to people with significant experience and influence, individuals who have been there and done that, and who are willing to share their ideas and thinking with me, allowing me to draw from their experience and insights.

In the early days, I didn't get it right. Looking back, there was a point when I realised that my network consisted only of people I worked with—it was very one-dimensional.

Now I am one of the most recognised finance professionals in Sydney finance circles, I have been asked to speak at numerous events and the connections have absolutely expanded my thinking and enabled me to perform even better in my current role.

I now have access to a broad and diverse range of individuals doing different things within the finance spectrum. It puts me in a unique position to understand what's going on in the industry at a broader level and also allows me to tap into the experience, expertise and insights of all these individuals.

Building a network that worked for me was critical—in fact, I think it has been a game changer.

Chax Poduri, senior finance executive, Hewlett Packard Enterprise

2

Rethink how you network now

One day I was enjoying lunch with my client Justine, who had recently been promoted to general manager of a large global property organisation. We were discussing the key deliverables of the new job along with the various levels of stakeholder management that were now required daily.

'It's hard work,' she explained. 'There's so much to do and I feel like I have no support, which is weird, right, because I have a big network.'

So we decided to dig a little deeper into this so-called great network.

- Who was in it?

- How had they helped her get to where she was right now?

- How were they going to continue to help her, given the demands of her new role and her aspirations for further career growth?

Up to this point Justine's network seemed to have been working for her. But her new role had created a new reality: not one person in her 500+ network could offer the advice, counsel and strategic thinking she needed at this more senior level with its associated challenges in relation to stakeholder management, organisational politics and game playing.

The reality was she had outgrown 20 per cent of her network, which was now working *against* her rather than *for* her.

Justine's experience is not unusual. Many of my clients reach a tipping point in their careers when they have to rethink themselves, their roles and their network. Most of us rise through the ranks based on our ability to deliver results and key performance indicators, and we clock up contacts as we go. Then suddenly we find that who we know becomes more important than what we know.

To have a network that continues to add value even as your status rises, you need to reassess and revise who you know, your goals and how you're going to achieve them.

You need people who understand the path you're on, especially when it changes.

What are your challenges now? What will they be in two years' time?

Justine had a choice to make. She could stay in stasis and 'play it by ear', or she could actively seek out individuals who could stretch her thinking and help her navigate the landscape in which she was now working.

Taking stock

So how are you actually networking right now? Only by understanding your current practice can you begin to start changing to what you need to be doing.

Although you may think you're networking, you're actually most likely doing it ineffectively. You may be part of a network group or two, have a list of contacts and a stack of connections across various social media platforms, but—and it's a big *but*—how many of your contacts do you *really* know? How many truly know you? How many of your contacts honestly care about you and your success? Do you understand each other's goals and aspirations? Are you doing things to help each other achieve them?

The reality is that networking as we know it tends to be shallow, superficial and ineffective. What you actually need for exponential growth and success is a network of transformational rather than transactional connections.

Figure 2.1 illustrates the evolution from ineffective to exponential networking, and the sections that follow examine the three stages of the journey to transformation.

Figure 2.1: ineffective to exponential networking

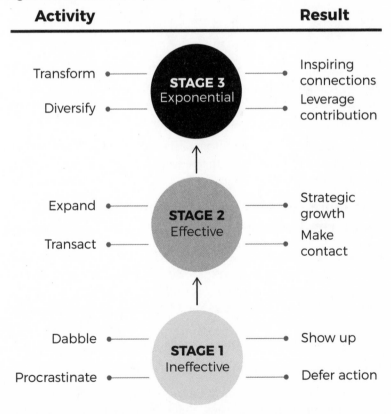

Stage 1: Ineffective

'I'm nervous about making connections ... I'm shy ... I'm an introvert.' These are among the common excuses advanced by those sitting at the bottom of the networking ladder. They've put the whole concept of networking in a box labelled 'Fear'.

Fear feeds on itself, eating away at our self-esteem, confidence and ability to share what's in our own head with anyone else. Worse still, this fear of engaging confidently means we inadvertently engage with failure. It's a bit like playing hide-and-seek on your own, or going to a party for one. Makes no sense, right?

If this is you then you're standing on the outside looking in. You probably think you don't have anyone you trust. Or maybe you are a perfectionist who can't relinquish control of small tasks so you're trying to do everything yourself.

If you've maxed out your mental credit limit, then you will have exhausted all of your resources just getting through the day to day. You've probably picked up this book thinking you'd like to expand your network or your company, or elevate your career, but even thinking about it is exhausting.

Confining yourself to the bottom of the ladder actually sets you up to become even more disconnected. It's a place that is inherently anti-growth and anti-change.

The more you stay put, the more isolated and alone you become.

Think of anyone who has stuck around in a job for way too long for fear of the unknown. Terina Allen, CEO of ARVis Institute, refers to this as 'job clinging' (LinkedIn, 19 September 2014). Allen defines job clingers as individuals who work in the same position or in the same company for a period of five or more years with little or no change in job title or salary.

The three key risks these job clingers face are:

1. getting paid less (see, for instance, 'Employees Who Stay in Companies Longer than Two Years Get Paid 50% Less', *Forbes*, 22 June 2014)

2. being overlooked for promotion

3. becoming less interesting to management and risking becoming irrelevant.

If you procrastinate or merely dabble at building a network, you face similar risks, including:

1. getting isolated from opportunities

2. going backwards in your career or losing your competitive edge

3. becoming irrelevant and invisible.

Procrastinating over networking, avoiding it altogether or simply showing up to events because you have to (and then leaving as quickly as possible) is not the road to success.

To start building any form of effective network you've got to *do something*. As with anything worthwhile in life, if you want to play the game you have to put in the effort, and first off that means turning up and being prepared to step out of your comfort zone. Before running a 100-metre sprint you have to know what your end goal is, so when that starting gun fires you simply go for it.

You need to make a conscious decision to explore other possibilities and people. It's time to face up to your fear, make the choice to go there and push through it. Dig deep and step out of the familiar and safe. It is only through taking action, and starting to transact with others, that this networking thing begins to deliver personal value. As the Chinese proverb says, 'Be not afraid of going slowly, be afraid of only standing still.'

WHO DO YOU KNOW?

- Are you an ineffective networker?
- Do you cower behind your computer, afraid of what will happen if you actually connect with someone?
- Do you procrastinate over networking?
- Do you merely dabble in networking events here and there?

Don't worry, this book will change all that!

Stage 2: Effective

Are you attending regular networking events already? Do you know people outside of your team, division or office? Do you connect with people on social media? Are you actively building a contact list?

If you answer 'yes' to these questions, then like most of us (including Justine at the beginning of this chapter) you are sitting comfortably in the 'effective' section of the networking ladder. You're busy transacting, making contacts and expanding your network.

Unlike the passivity typical at stage 1 of the model, behaviours in the second stage are more active and assertive. You probably don't need convincing that networking is a critical part of business growth. However, you likely think that getting to know the people you need and building business leads is simply a numbers game. You are convinced, consciously or unconsciously, that at some point these leads will result in a sale, referral or recommendation.

Put simply, you're leaving it to chance.

Though you're connecting with like-minded people, finding individuals who can support you personally through learning and information, or operationally through lead generation and business development, you don't really have any control over this.

You do engage with networking groups, industry events or personal development programs. Most likely you've been a part of these so long you know everyone's name.

We know that eating a box of chocolates every night won't reduce our waistline, that watching hours of inane reality TV won't feed our intellect and that sitting on our butt hour after hour won't give our body the exercise it needs. In the same way, connecting only with the same individuals or groups will limit your potential. When you're comfortable, nothing is really working for you, and eventually (as Justine discovered), this passivity will start to work against you.

In his classic book *How to Win Friends and Influence People*, Dale Carnegie argued that you can make 'more friends in two months by becoming interested in other people than you can in two years by trying to get other people interested in you'. This is all very transactional and transacting is a numbers game, in which your engagement with others is often shallow and purely operational. At this stage you're focused on 'What's in it for me?' *Is this going to be a business lead? Can I sell to this person? Will knowing you give me more brand exposure?*

If you really want to progress in your career, you need to evolve into someone who gives back as well as takes. Stage 2 is just the beginning when it comes to strategically building an influential network.

WHO DO YOU KNOW?

- Do you consider yourself an effective networker?
- Do you know lots of people and attend regular networking events?
- Do you have a stack of business cards, Facebook friends, Twitter followers and LinkedIn connections?
- Do you make regular efforts to expand your network?

Maybe it's time to step your life and your career up a notch.

Stage 3: Exponential

Up to this point your networking has consisted of building contacts who may be able to:

- help you do the job you have
- support your immediate personal development needs
- help you achieve your current key business goals.

At the Exponential stage you focus on the *quality* of the people you know rather than their number. Here networking is about:

1. diversifying your connections, seeking out people who challenge your thinking, planning and direction

2. finding individuals whose functions differ from yours, who work in other industries or at a different hierarchical level

3. accessing other skills and expertise you don't have

4. becoming curious about possibility and opportunity

5. connecting in order to develop a deeper understanding of yourself and others

6. becoming deliberate and focused in your actions and endeavours

7. investing time and effort to engage for your own and others' success

8. embracing the power of reciprocity

9. pushing boundaries

10. building a network where you are smack bang in the centre.

Building an effective and powerful network is about much more than finding your 'tribe'. It requires a breadth of contacts and skills so you open yourself up to more possibilities and embrace opportunities you would never find in a homogeneous group. You may not always agree with your tribe, but that's just why it's important. Questioning leads to further awareness and knowledge.

Building a network of transformational connections involves embracing differing levels of expertise, age and experience.

It is about immersing yourself in a conversation that spans industries and functions, with no limits on the range and depth of discussion. Corporate leaders, creatives, coaches, entrepreneurs and lawyers, for example, solving problems together. It's about colourful conversations, sharing different perspectives and broader views.

In 'The Network Secrets of Great Change Agents' (*HBR*, July 2013), Julie Battilana and Tiziana Casciaro suggest that building a network at this level isn't so much about where someone ranks in a company's formal hierarchy; more importantly, it's about how well that person understands and mobilises information, insight and other individuals to effect change.

Whether you are at the top of an organisation or just starting out, a leader in your field or a novice, understanding the opportunity that exists when you own your network and act strategically, transformationally, is the key to success.

As networking master Keith Ferrazzi puts it, 'Your network is your destiny ... we are the people we interact with.'

WHO DO YOU KNOW?

- Do you think you're an exponential networker?
- Is your network diverse, open and transformational?
- Do you have people in your network who have skills you don't?
- Does your network challenge your thinking, build curiosity, push you further than you would go alone?

Really? Then something's still not working if you're reading this book.

From transaction to transformation

As we've just explored, rethinking your network starts with your moving away from transactional networking, the traditional type of networking, and towards transformational networking. There is, however, a place for both types of networking, and it's important you understand the differences between them so you engage appropriately in the right context.

Figure 2.2 (overleaf) summarises the differences between transactional and transformational networking.

Figure 2.2: transact versus transform

Transact	vs	Transform
Business building	**PURPOSE**	Personal growth
Quantity	**FOCUS**	Quality
Shallow	**DEPTH OF CONNECTION**	Deep
Closed and same	**LOCATION**	Open and diverse
Stable	**BEHAVIOUR**	Leverage
Give or take	**ENGAGEMENT**	Mutual value exchange
Out of control	**OWNERSHIP**	In control
Operational	**RESULT**	Strategic and operational

Transactional networking does matter and definitely still has a role to play, but you need to be clear on what its role is. The old-school approach of transacting relies on status and quantity—your own talent, previous successes, the title on your business card, the letters you have after your name and the number of people you know. As a numbers game, it is absolutely essential for business growth, lead and sales generation.

Transformational networking, on the other hand, engages your personal network on a deeper level, and matters more. It is about putting you right in the middle of a network that connects you to people and information that matters for your growth and personal success.

networking = transaction = business growth
network = transform = personal growth

It's time to transform your network.

Think narrow, go deep

In the 1990s British anthropologist Robin Dunbar suggested there's a limit to the number of relationships human beings can comfortably maintain—150, to be precise. It is possible for us to maintain stable relationships with this many others, remembering their names, keeping in contact, doing each other favours. Any more than this, he proposed, leads to fragmentation into subgroups and smaller tribes.

This theory has been challenged a number of times, including most recently by Michael Simmons in 'How Big Should Your Network Be' (*Forbes*, 2 January 2014). Zvi Band, the founder of Contactually, a relationship management tool, argues that in our highly digi-connected world, 'current software can extend Dunbar's number by at least two to three times'.

It makes sense that when there are too many members in your group or tribe other subgroups and tribes will start forming, and that this will undermine goals such as sales generation and reduce your network's influence and impact.

I suggest also that momentum begins with a significantly smaller circle of influence (starting with four and then expanding to 12, as we will see in the following chapters), with you situated securely in the centre. A small group of people providing quality thinking and models of behaviour, pushing you further than you could ever go alone — it is here that transformational connections are made possible. This is where you start to change the game, to make the impossible possible, to inspire others to act, connect and dream.

We're all time poor, so it's crucial that we select those we invite into our small circle carefully and strategically. Take a long hard look at your network. How many people are there? What impact are they really having? Where do you sit on the figure 2.1 networking ladder? Are you procrastinating, dabbling, transacting, expanding, diversifying or transforming? Chances are, like most of us, you are somewhere in the middle and that means it's time to change.

As we've seen, we need to stop trying to be too many things for too many people through merely transacting. It's time to exchange value to mutual advantage, to develop trust along with connected visions and goals. Only by focusing on our core network can we develop the potential to affect a wider audience. Opportunity and growth happen when we zero in and go narrow, developing connections that matter and build our confidence.

Building a network that works requires understanding the connections we must make, as opposed to those we *are* making. We have to let go of our obsession with quantity and learn the art of strategic networking.

Successful networking hinges on who you know and the resulting collaboration that happens between those people. In *Never Eat Alone*, Keith Ferrazzi concludes, 'Success in life = (the people you meet) + (what you create together).' The real power, as we'll examine in the next chapter, lies in working together as a collective.

Joining forces

Lisa McAdams is a domestic violence workplace strategist and solutions consultant based in Sydney. When she started on her entrepreneurial journey she was alone and had to network like crazy.

'If you act with integrity the right network can supercharge the speed you grow your business,' says Lisa. 'There are people there when you win and there are people there to pick you up when you don't.'

Lisa found her tribe with the LBDGroup, a network of smart, commercial and results-driven businesswomen and entrepreneurs. She built around her a network of individuals who worked together to bring her vision to fruition. She engaged strategisers, digital experts and corporate networkers, as well as those who fed her confidence and self-belief. Lisa is now recognised as a leader in domestic violence solutions.

Lisa adds, 'Business became a joint venture of contacts and capabilities. Knowledge is shared and advice given. My network consists of my people, my team, a group who support each other. They will celebrate with me but then in the next breath say, "Right, what's next? Are you focused?" They push me to become more instead of creating a new comfort zone.'

3

Transform to a collective network

In Suzanne Collins' science fiction trilogy *The Hunger Games*, one boy and one girl aged between 12 and 18 are selected by lottery from each of the 12 districts to fight in a murderous televised game of survival.

When 16-year-old Katniss Everdeen strategically outflanks both the other contestants and the organisers using as her weapons compassion and collaboration rather than anger and competition, she not only wins the contest but also becomes the symbol of revolution.

Alone Katniss is no threat. But when she joins forces with other strategists and game players of diverse talents, her influence and impact increase exponentially. She carefully selects individuals who add strength where she is weak, so collectively they form one super-power capable of overthrowing the dictatorship that has long ruled their universe.

As with much dystopian fiction, there are clear lessons to be drawn from the story, the foremost of which is that we can only achieve so much on our own, but when we align ourselves strategically with the right people we have the potential to create change and transform the game of life.

The eye of the storm

No matter what stage of your career you are at, in today's world of constant challenge, change and busyness you simply will not be able to move fast enough on your own. And sitting on your hands and waiting for the world to help you is like sitting in the middle of a tornado.

You have to take ownership and responsibility for your own decisions and direction, or risk getting sucked up and spat out in a totally unexpected place.

You must learn to build a strategic network that works for you.

To survive the whirlwind, you need to unlearn everything you have been told to date about networking. Ask yourself: *Who is in my network now? Who should be in my network now? How can we work together as a group to effect change?* Author Shannon Adler put it beautifully when she said, 'When you invite people to share in your miracle, you create future allies during rough weather.'

Richard Branson said, 'No-one is successful alone.' Building a network for personal growth in the 21st century hinges on connecting and collaborating with the right people, openly sharing knowledge and insights with individuals who understand, at a deeper level, our goals and aspirations and who nurture a collective interest in our own growth and that of the whole group. It is only when we learn to move together that we start to move faster.

People power

Every year more than 2500 people gather for five days in Davos, Switzerland, to discuss global challenges at the World Economic Forum. This meeting brings together many of the world's most influential people: presidents, prime ministers, business and financial leaders, journalists and celebrities, from Al Gore to Bill Gates, Bono to Paulo Coelho.

The role of the World Economic Forum, established in 1971 by the Austrian politician Klaus Schwab, is.

> to connect the dots, to provide leaders with a space to proactively focus on the future and develop a forward-looking strategic view in a world that is increasingly interconnected and, at the same time, absorbed by the challenges of the past[2]

It is the very act of bringing these diverse people together that makes the meeting of minds at Davos so vital. As Schwab put it, 'Progress happens by bringing together people from all walks of life who have the drive and the influence to make positive change.'

Connecting and collaborating with others of diverse skills and experience (as Katniss did) helps to compensate for our own personal weaknesses. We all have individual strengths, passions and experience to draw on. But if we dwell only on our strengths and ignore our weaknesses we risk getting left behind.

Connecting only with like-minded people, though, which happens a lot when you're busy transacting with people (as we saw in the previous chapter), stifles our growth.

It's natural that we connect most with others in our own organisation or vocation. Lawyers spend time with others in the legal profession, small business people share their business challenges with others working in a similar area, graduates share their early career frustrations with fellow graduates. At some point, however, this conversation becomes oversaturated and we get 'over it'.

The key is to connect with diverse people, because through diversity you build competitive advantage.

What area are you weak or lacking in? Make a concerted effort to seek out and connect with someone who is strong in that particular area.

Value is a two-way street

In their book *The Go-Giver*, authors Bob Burg and John David Mann tell the story of an ambitious young man, Joe, who yearns for success. Joe is a go-getter with clear goals and success targets, but the harder he works the further away from his goals he finds himself.

One day, desperate to land a sale at the end of a bad sales quarter, Joe approaches Pinder, a legendary consultant, for advice. Pinder introduces Joe to his diverse network of trusted colleagues representing a wide variety of industries and jobs.

Pinder's friends encourage Joe to embrace the power of giving, of sharing insights and knowledge with others. Joe learns about the opportunity generated when we put others' interests before our own, when we consistently look for ways to add value for others, when we network for mutual benefit rather than seeking advantage only for ourselves.

At the heart of a successful network lies the concept of value exchange—a mutually beneficial process that relies on more than just a transaction.

Value exchange is about two or more individuals sharing insights, connections, knowledge and ideas. This is where sales and market value increase exponentially.

In his book *Give and Take*, Adam Grant suggests the individuals most likely to rise to the top are often 'Givers', those who contribute most to others. 'Takers', who seek to gain as much as possible from others, and 'Matchers', who aim to give and take in equal amounts, rarely experience the same success.

In addition, something magical happens when 'Givers' thrive:

> Givers succeed in a way that creates a ripple effect, enhancing the success of people around them. Every time we interact with another person at work, we have a choice to make: do we try to claim as much value as we can, or contribute value without worrying about what we receive in return?

Victor Webster writes, 'If you throw a pebble into the water on one side of the ocean, it can create a tidal wave on the other side.' An effective network creates a ripple effect of growth and opportunity. Social psychologists call it the 'Law of Reciprocity'; others recognise it in the social convention of 'what goes around comes around'. No matter who you are, and what your title or area of responsibility, every connection you make has an impact. Each connection and interaction creates a ripple, which leads to countless others down the line.

Networking is like throwing a pebble into a pond. Individually we are all capable of creating some kind of movement, but working together we create ripples that build momentum and impact as they spread.

It's not a competition

The business world has become increasingly competitive, but networking doesn't need to be about competition. Let me explain.

The Johari Window model, developed in 1955 by Joseph Luft and Harry Ingham, was aimed at helping improve understanding between individuals. It was based on the idea that you can only build trust in others by disclosing information about yourself, and that feedback from others helps us learn and improve ourselves.

Our network is built along similar lines: by sharing parts of ourselves, we find that others are willing to share with us. We are all in this together.

Many entrepreneurs I meet spend more time worrying about whether they will find the right collaborative opportunities than about what their competitors are doing. They understand the value that exists in working together, sharing intelligence and insight to create new opportunities, products and markets.

Your success will be compounded when you collaborate openly, willingly and with complete, honest, full disclosure.

Focus on the competition, obsess about what they are doing and what you think you should be doing, and you'll go round and round in circles to no effect.

In my book *From Me to We: Why commercial collaboration will future proof business, leaders and personal success*, I discuss in detail the seven re-connect principles that drive collaborative working practices. One of the key principles is value exchange.

Some worry that participating in a small, mutually beneficial network means engaging with our competition, and that they'll find out about our weaknesses and use them against us. There is no doubt in my mind that the opportunity offered by mutual value exchange is far greater than the risk of competition.

I am not so naive as to claim that competition doesn't happen. Sure, at some point you may feel like someone took one of your ideas and ran with it. Business may even feel like it's getting personal as people piggyback off your thinking. I know this from personal experience. It can be devastating — if you allow it to be. But that's the key: it will crush you only if you allow it to.

In the early days of my business my initial conviction was reinforced by a growing client base and healthy bank account. I was focused, determined, well and truly in the zone. I knew what I was doing, knew my bigger why and how I was going to achieve my goals. No-one could stop me.

Then, after the first 18 months, I opened my eyes to what was going on around me. I became increasingly aware of the competition in my field. I listened to external commentary, which pulled me in multiple directions. Instead of focusing on the positives that stared me in the face, I started paying attention to the downsides of what I was doing. The result? I started to go round and round in circles, frozen in time.

The lesson? If you focus on what the competition are doing and what they might think of you, you will make no progress at all. But when you focus on your network and goals, collaborating with people who will help drive your growth, the positive results will flow.

Ingredients of a powerful network

In 'Building an Innovation Factory' (*HBR*, May 2000), Andrew Hargadon and Robert I. Sutton discuss how to broker and capture good ideas for true and long-lasting effect. One of the companies studied is IDEO, an international design and consulting firm founded in Palo Alto, California. The most respected people at IDEO are:

1. part pack rat—they have great private collections of stuff
2. part librarian—they know who knows what
3. part Good Samaritan—they go out of their way to share what they know and to help others.

Approach your network in a similar way. You need a personal:

1. *board of advisers* that brings out the best in you
2. *intelligence bank* that sustains you over the long term
3. *marketing machine* that champions you and your cause.

Let's look at each of these in a bit more detail.

1. Your personal board of advisers

American entrepreneur and motivational speaker Jim Rohn says, 'You are the average of the five people you surround yourself with.' In this book, I'm recommending you surround yourself with a minimum of four people, with 12 as an ideal.

It is essential that you build your own intimate network covering key skills. Think of this as your own personal board of advisers who add to your ideas and bring out the best in you at every stage of your career.

We invest in personal trainers for our fitness goals, financial advisers for our investment goals, even meditation teachers for our work–life goals. It is just as important to invest in a personal board of advisers as a sounding board and safety net to explore your ideas and plan your next career steps. Your boardroom provides encouragement, support and inspiration.

So who do you need to surround yourself with to inspire you and help you achieve more? Who do you need around you to provide support and to challenge your thinking? Who helps you test ideas, proposals or product innovations before you launch to a wider audience?

2. Your personal intelligence bank

Think of building your network as creating a personal 'intelligence bank' in which you invest in the same way a child makes regular coin deposits into their piggybank. The heavier the piggybank becomes, the more they have saved to purchase something important to them later. Invest in the right people with the right skills and it will pay dividends over the long term.

Appreciate the value of an intelligence bank and the potential of the value exchange. Perhaps suggest to individuals in your network that you 'swap' a skill for a skill, so you each learn something you previously had no knowledge of.

Build your intelligence bank by embracing the strengths and skills of others around you, and in this way create more opportunity to influence others.

3. Your personal marketing machine

This is about forming a personal cheer squad who help you to create momentum because they believe in you.

Troye Sivan is a South African–born Australian singer, songwriter, actor, and YouTube personality. An early adopter of YouTube (2007), Troye began by uploading videos of himself singing cover songs. Five years later he started posting more personal video blogs, and in 2013 he released the track 'The Fault in Our Stars', which went viral thanks to his legion of online fans. EMI noticed and approached him with a record deal—the marketing machine hit the ground running.

In 2014, with more than 4 million subscribers and over 241 million total video views, *Time* magazine named Troye one of the top 25 most influential teens. Troye's significant fan base has become his marketing machine. And he has a close, tight-knit network that supports his bigger-picture vision.

Without a marketing machine around you, your ability to create change and build engagement and influence is limited. To really drive your net worth and influence, you have to tap into what's around you.

Focus drives momentum

It's easy to put off committing to health and fitness plans or personal development goals and just blob out in front of the latest reality TV show. These days the only way we seem to be able to keep focused is if our goal involves fundraising for a charity event.

Sometimes it's hard, really hard, to stay focused in the zone. Competitors do something, the media shows us something, friends say something and we either listen or ignore it.

This is the beauty of having your personal advisory board, your intelligence bank, your marketing machine. They understand your bigger-picture goals and dreams. They are your sounding board and help shape your thinking. This network will help you stay in the zone and develop resilience during the tough times, and will fuel your hunger and belief.

Your network will keep your focus laser sharp and help guide you towards the decisions you need to make to move forward. As American sociologist Ronald Burt puts it, 'Instead of better glasses, your network gives you better eyes.'

It's up to you to turn your focus inwards, to look strategically at who is in your current network and who can help you get to where you're going. Which is what we explore in part II.

Collective power

Suzie Hoitink is the founder of Clear Complexions Clinics. In addition to raising a family of two competitive sports–mad teenage girls, Suzie has created a solid business with a loyal client base. She is recognised in the skin care industry as a thought leader and expert commentator.

Clear Complexions had significant TV exposure, and Suzie had clarity and conviction around her brand's unique positioning along with a rock-solid vision for the future.

However, there was a problem.

The business was limited geographically because it was based in one Australian city, Canberra. Suzie's network had supported her both personally and professionally through the growth of her business, but if she was to achieve any future success, she would have to push herself out of her comfort zone and seek help from a new network.

'It was time to push into new states and grow the brand, but I had totally underestimated how difficult this would be,' Suzie recalls. 'After many expensive mistakes and the uncertainty that comes with it, I looked to what connections I had to help.

It became very clear that my networking circle needed to grow to be relevant to where I was now and where I wanted to be.'

Bit by bit, Suzie strategically regained control of her network. She contacted people in other parts of Australia and began expanding her personal reach, connecting with people with skills that weren't necessarily in her area of expertise.

She sought out new teachers, mentors and promoters. She reviewed and evolved her support crew. She embraced an expanded and connected network, and pushed herself personally beyond her comfort zone.

This new, diversified and expanded network challenged her decisions, stretched her thinking and inspired her to think bigger. And it paid off.

Her business expanded, in 2013 she was nominated for and won a Telstra Businesswomen's Award, and her business continues to grow and expand, moving her closer to her bigger vision.

PART II
WHO

You now understand the difference between transactional and transformational networking. You also know that you absolutely must embrace transformational networking to have any hope of building a strategic and successful network.

The real question is: Where do you start?

How do you know if the network you have now is the right one or will come even close to helping you achieve your goals?

Who are the people you need in your network?

Who is hindering your success?

How do you identify who is missing from your network?

Part I outlines the essential background, insight and knowledge you need to transform your network. In part II you get more hands-on!

We'll work through some exercises together to assess the network you currently have and explain what you need. You'll discover the Nexus, which comprises your Core Four when it comes to building your network.

Then you'll take it a step further and meet the 12 key people and personalities you need to take control of your network and work towards a successful network.

You'll see that the choices you make regarding the people you spend time with determine the quality of conversations you have, the insights you have access to, the calibre of the decisions you make, and the attributes, mindset and behaviours you will portray.

There are four key stages to building a small, smart and strategic network:

1. SORT. What sort of network do you have now? Do you even have a network? We'll assess your current situation in chapter 4.

2. SEARCH. Who are your Core Four? Who are the four key individuals you must have in your network? You'll meet them in chapter 5.

3. SEEK. Who are the 12 key people and personalities that make up your small, smart and strategic network? In chapter 6 we'll break the Core Four down further and introduce the 12 connections you need to accelerate your success.

4. SINK. Who is in your network that shouldn't be? Who are the 12 Shadow Archetypes? In chapter 7 you'll learn that tough love is essential to a strategic network.

So now let's find out who you need in your network.

4

Sort through your current network

As discussed in part I, you probably already have some sort of network, whether it's working effectively for you or not. But even if you hate the idea of networking and find yourself on the bottom rungs of the networking ladder introduced in chapter 2, you will have some contacts, friends and acquaintances, or will at least have connected with them on social media.

Your powerful web of resources, connections and opportunities begins right here, in and around your own backyard. The people you see every day at work or on the weekend, or meet from time to time at functions, not to mention your clients and suppliers—they are likely the starting point when it comes to identifying who is in your current network.

You now understand that more opportunity is created when you are strategic about how you network and who you network with. This is what enables you to grow exponentially. It's where you'll leverage contributions and build inspired connections that matter.

You are going to need to step up and step out, to reach out and diversify your network to include those with skills, talent and qualities that feed your growth, to transform your current into your future, to connect with those who will fast-track your success.

Edmund Lee gets it right when he says, 'Surround yourself with the dreamers and the doers, the believers and thinkers, but most of all, surround yourself with those who see the greatness within you, even when you don't see it yourself.'

These are the questions you'll be asking yourself:

- Where do I start?

- What types of people do I need in my network?

- How do I know if I already have these people in my network?

- And if I don't, how do I find them?

So let's start by addressing some of these questions.

Back to basics

To progress from a transactional network to a strategic and transformational one, you've got to first assess who is in your network right now. This requires some sorting.

The SORT process will help you:

- identify who is in your network right now

- assess the true diversity and integration of your network

- highlight any gaps that may exist.

Think of this as a top-level triage health check. You're going to zero in on what your network looks like right now and understand how it's currently serving you, assessing how these people are helping or hindering you when it comes to your goals and aspirations. Only once you have processed your existing network in this way can you get serious about your next steps, which will culminate in your seeking out those people who are missing from your network.

There are two steps in the SORT phase:

1. identify

2. assess.

Let's work through each step in detail together.

Step 1: Identify

First up, who's in your network?

You might be surprised at how hard this simple question can actually be to answer! This isn't about doing a brain dump of everyone you know—or getting out your phone to check your contacts or your Facebook feed (as a lot of people in my workshops do). As you will soon see, there is a big difference between people you know and people who add value to your life and career and therefore have a right to belong in your current core network.

When assessing your network, think about the individuals you currently go to or rely on for support, information, advice, inspiration or simply as a sounding board for your thinking. This might include your partner, colleagues, friends, family members, or your existing or former boss.

As you think about your network, consider how you interact and connect, and what exchange of information or support happens.

You've got to understand your current network before you can change or improve it. So who is in your network right now?

WHO DO YOU KNOW?

- List 10 to 15 people you consider to be crucial in your life and your network.

- Fill out the SORT Worksheet in figure 4.1 (overleaf, or download or print it from **janinegarner.com.au/resources** if you prefer).

Struggling to come up with even 10? Then you're on the right track! This process is not as easy as you might think. You're starting to discover how many people you know, but how few add real value to your network.

Figure 4.1: SORT Worksheet

IDENTIFY YOUR NETWORK

ASSESS YOUR NETWORK

What's their name?	What's their gender?		How do you know them?	Where do they live?
	M	F		
1	○	○		
2	○	○		
3	○	○		
4	○	○		
5	○	○		
6	○	○		
7	○	○		
8	○	○		
9	○	○		
10	○	○		
11	○	○		
12	○	○		
13	○	○		
14	○	○		
15	○	○		

Step 2: Assess

Now we're going to delve a bit deeper in order to assess how diverse your network really is. Consider the following three questions:

1. What is the gender make-up of your network?

2. What similarities are apparent among the individuals in your network?

3. Where is everyone located?

Let's examine these questions in some detail.

1. What is the gender make-up of your network?

Is your list evenly balanced between males and females, or does it err heavily to one side of the gender equation? Are both genders even represented?

I find it amazing when facilitating this exercise how many times my clients have realised they have all men or all women in their network. I've lost track of the number of studies that link a gender-balanced workplace and leadership team to positive business performance and employee engagement. The same can be said for your network.

Lisa Torres, a sociology professor at George Washington University, and Matt L. Huffman, a sociology researcher at the University of California, Irvine, studied groups of men and women and tracked census data to identify patterns in the way the sexes network. In their 2002 study 'Social Networks and Job Search Outcomes Among Male and Female Professional, Technical, and Managerial Workers', they confirmed the truth of the saying 'birds of a feather flock together'.

They found that both men and women have a tendency to gravitate to networks of their own gender. This sheds some light on why men continue to hold the majority of senior positions in most organisations across the world. When it comes to job openings and career opportunities, we naturally share these first within our network, and in this case it's in a network of mainly male colleagues. Women often won't hear about these opportunities until after they've done the rounds in the all-male network.

William T. Bielby, a professor emeritus of sociology at the University of Illinois at Chicago, explains:

> Women have tended to be better connected overall, but they and many of their female contacts tend to work in more female-dominated jobs. So their networks may be wider but not reach to as high a level as men's, who tend to be better connected, particularly in getting professional news, to more high-status people.

So being connected is not enough; you need to build a diverse network to create a ripple effect for change. A broad range of different thinking and ideas generates competitive advantage. It is from differences of opinion, ideas and thoughts that opportunities emerge.

WHO DO YOU KNOW?

- Tick the gender of each person you've listed in the SORT worksheet.
- How many women do you have in your immediate network? How many men?
- Is there an obvious lack of balance and diversity?

2. What similarities exist in your network?

How many of the people in your list are attached to the same company, community, sporting club, co-working space, university, church, mothers' group or other group? How many are your relatives or friends? How many do you work with, perhaps in the same department? How many are at the same seniority level?

It's common to find ourselves gravitating towards the people we see regularly, spend most time with or have most contact with, so it's likely they will be the first ones to spring to mind at step 1 of the SORT process. We often find it easier to connect with people who have the same knowledge, background or work focus as us. We tend to be drawn to clusters of 'sameness', staying in our comfort zone.

When we start working in a new job or role we mix mainly with co-workers in our department or those at a similar seniority level as us. As we stay longer in a company, opportunities arise to expand our network simply through promotion and tenure. We may be thrown into roles that force us to collaborate with other departments or companies. We may work with virtual teams including people based interstate and overseas.

How many people do you know outside your area of expertise? Do your connections actually suggest you are working in a silo?

WHO DO YOU KNOW?

- How do you know the people on your list?
- Use one word to sum up where you met or the relationship you have with each individual you identified in the previous step, and add that word to your SORT worksheet.
- Do you notice any patterns of sameness or similarity?
- How many people on your list are from similar organisations or groups?

3. Where is everyone located?

Knowing people in different areas of the same business as you or with differing levels of expertise increases the diversity of your network. Including among your contacts people from different geographical locations does the same. Think about where the people in your list are based. Are they in the same city, state or country? Do you have people in your network who live overseas?

While we may not always be geographically close, thanks to technology we have never been more closely connected or had more opportunities to communicate regardless of geography. We should therefore not discount individuals from our network based on their location, whether it be a different city or state, or even a different continent; in fact, we should embrace such opportunities.

Your organisation may have offices around the world. It's likely you sometimes travel, either for work or on a holiday. These trips create valuable opportunities for meeting people and nurturing connections in different locations. How many times when travelling have you bumped into someone you've swapped business cards with at an airport or in a local café, for example?

So does the reality of your network reflect the reality of the diverse world in which you live?

WHO DO YOU KNOW?

- Note down on the SORT worksheet where each of your connections is located.

- What do you notice?

- Are they based in the same city, state or country?

- Does this accurately reflect all the different people you know in different parts of the world?

What did you discover from the SORT process? For example, do you have mostly males in your network? Or females? Is your network made up mostly of your friends, family members or current colleagues? Are most individuals in your network co-workers, clients or customers? Do they all live in the same city as you or are they spread out interstate?

Getting your network right is all about getting started. And that's exactly what you've just done, so good on you!

As you've learned, a strong strategic network relies on one key principle—diversity. A diverse network spans gender, age, experience, culture, industries, organisations and geographical locations.

Imagine you're having a party. If you invite all the people on your list, how many of them would already know each other, having met before, or have heard you talk about them? The more they know each other, the more closed and tight your network is. If hardly any of your connections know each other, then you probably have a pretty open and diverse network.

Are you open or closed?

Like most of the people who do this exercise for the first time, you've probably discovered you have a fairly closed network. This means you surround yourself with people who are similar to you. Most of them do the same sorts of things you do, think like you, value the same things; they may even do the same job or at least be at the same seniority level or life stage.

An implicit level of trust and loyalty operates in this kind of tribe, and it naturally creates an environment of mutual value exchange. However, if you're forever surrounded by people who say and think the same thing, then you begin to accept this as the norm and dismiss anything else as deviant. You don't question where you are in life or how you're going to get to the next level. You don't push yourself; you just accept the status quo. You do the same things, go to the same restaurants, have the same conversations and stay in the same job. Put simply, you put your blindfold on.

In her book *Wilful Blindness*, Margaret Heffernan discusses how as human beings we naturally associate with like-minded people. Our challenge is that we are deeply influenced by the norms and standards of those around us, such that our brain edits out facts that aren't in line with that world view. Heffernan explains, 'When we are wilfully blind there is information we could know and should know but don't because it makes us feel better not to.' This is why a closed network of contacts can create a blinkered approach to networking and limit opportunities, options and ideas.

At its extreme this attitude leads to *groupthink*, a term originally coined by social psychologist Irving Janis in 1972. Evidence of this tendency can be seen everywhere, from political parties and sporting teams to schoolyards and the media.

Sticking with the same people, with the same in-group, is safe and boring. You might expect that a diverse group means you'll always be wrestling with a lot of different, conflicting opinions, but the opposite tends to happen.

A more open and diverse network often means that individuals in your network often do not know one another and may have different values and beliefs. This greater diversity can have a profound, far-reaching impact.

An open network encourages diversity of opinion and insight, with access to other ways of doing things stretching out-of-the-box thinking.

If your network is too open, however, managing it can be exhausting. Keeping up with everyone, maintaining different conversations at different levels, is demanding. You'll wear different hats with different people, and feel like a chameleon as you morph to fit in with whomever you are connecting with at that time. There is no continuity of discussion, and perhaps no shared insight or opinion. In the end, all you can do is flit from one conversation to another while never actually moving forward. Social media is the best example of an open network at the extreme, with millions of people maintaining irredeemably shallow connections online.

Balance is the answer

We also get the balance of our network wrong when we choose to keep work and home totally separate from one another, convinced that this is what work–life balance is all about. This may have worked when we lived in the world of 9 to 5, when we switched off at the end of the day to head home and live our isolated family life, but things have changed dramatically since technology infiltrated our lives.

We are now contactable 24/7, with every aspect of our lives on show (if we choose it) online. Where, how and when we work will continue to evolve. The boundary between work and home life is more and more fluid, and the effort to keep work and home totally separate is draining and futile. It's time to stick with one hat. It's time to integrate our network so it can become truly diverse.

The ideal scenario is a balanced and integrated network that bridges smaller diverse groups and is:

- cross-hierarchical
- cross-functional
- cross-organisational.

A balanced, interconnected network enables diversity of learning, reduces bias in decision making, and increases opportunity for personal growth and opportunity.

Businesswoman and accountant Melissa Browne exemplifies this perfectly. When I interviewed her about the diversity of her network she said:

> When I first started my accounting firm I imitated other successful accounting firms. That's how I presumed you ran a successful firm. What I quickly realised was how limiting that was to growth, cash flow and the opportunity to attract clients because I wasn't offering anything different.
>
> So I looked outside my world to what other interesting entrepreneurs were doing: fitness gurus, stylists, military coaches, fashion brands, franchises and more.
>
> I believe if you want to be a clone of someone else then look to your industry but if you want to innovate, you

need to look outside your own world. I join tribes and organisations where business owners aren't the same as me. I make a point of being uncomfortable so I can continue to challenge any unconscious bias.

Inwards, outwards and upwards

Knowing what you want in terms of your goals and aspirations is one thing, but achieving them is something else again. The process you've just completed is the start of your journey to achieve greater success.

It's only by looking inwards that we start to look outwards and then move upwards. Some people find this a confronting idea; for others, it blows their mind!

It's important to remember that this is not a one-off, set-and-forget process. Your life and career goals and the people around you change constantly based on where you are in life and at work. So your network must constantly evolve too.

That's why you'll find you will need to access this book's website resources time and time again to work through this process and the ones in the following chapters. I recommend you keep coming back and assessing your network long after you've finished reading this book.

Now you've completed the SORT process on your existing network, it's time to shift focus to assess whether you are really connecting with the people that matter to achieving your goals — it's time to build your network, your own Nexus of Core Four and ultimately the 12 key people who will fast-track your success.

As you work through chapters 5 and 6, you'll keep coming back to your network list as you ask yourself who you already have in your network and who is missing. But to do this properly, strategically, first you need to meet the Core Four individuals that form your Nexus, the essential heart of your network. That's what we'll look at in the following chapter.

Search for your Core Four

Four is a magic number.

Just as there are four essential elements that work together in the universe (fire, water, air and earth), there are four critical roles in business. These are:

1. Chief Executive Officer — vision and strategy = fire

2. Chief Operating Officer — resources and operations = water

3. Chief Information Officer — new thinking = air

4. Chief Financial Officer — performance and results = earth.

In sport, every successful team consolidates vision, talent, ideas and action across the four key roles of owner, manager, coach and captain. In 'The Making of a Corporate Athlete' (*HBR*, January 2001), Jim Loehr and Tony Schwartz propose that an individual optimises their talents and skills through the balance of four key areas: physical, emotional, mental and spiritual.

Many popular TV shows hinge on four key characters. Think of Vince, Drama, Eric and Turtle in *Entourage*. In *Sex and the City* the four lead characters can be broken down into four distinct personalities:

1. Samantha—rebel, lover, fanatic (fire)

2. Charlotte—fantasist, carer, nurturer (water)

3. Carrie—dreamer, writer, thinker (air)

4. Miranda—butt-kicker, go-getter, realist (earth).

Novelist J. K. Rowling based her Harry Potter series on the chronicles and adventures of four houses at Hogwarts School of Wizardry, whose heroes included (and could be exemplified by):

1. Gryffindor—adventurous, courageous, brave and determined (fire)

2. Hufflepuff—hard working, dedicated, patient and supportive (water)

3. Ravenclaw—intelligent, wise, curious and focused (air)

4. Slytherin—ambitious, results-oriented and cunning (earth).

It is said that the mind can generally juggle four different items of information at the same time; any more and confusion sets in.

From books and TV shows to the boardroom, *four* works. It also works in networking. When it comes to building a strategic and smart network (your Nexus), you need to first of all establish a 'Core Four'—this is your starting point before you move on to building the 12 key people we will meet in the next chapter.

Four allows balance, diversity, dedication and success. And four is the magic number when it comes to the start of a successful network.

Your Core Four—the starting point of your network

Who are your Core Four? These four personality types should be your starting point when building a network. We will expand further on the four categories in the next chapter when we look at the 12 key people you need. (The types are loosely based on the personality archetype work of psychologist Carl Jung.)

The Core Four (as shown in figure 5.1) that you must have to start your strategic network are:

1. **Promoter**—makes noise about potential possibilities and inspires you to dream big (your fire)

2. **Pit Crew**—keeps you on track, nurtures you and prevents untoward emotions from getting the better of you (your water)

3. **Teacher**—helps you develop knowledge, wisdom and foresight (your air)

4. **Butt-kicker**—accelerates your journey, pushes you to do more and holds you accountable for your actions (your earth).

Figure 5.1: the Nexus—your Core Four

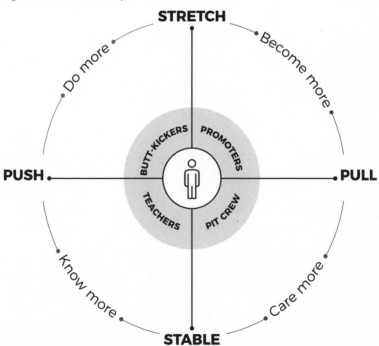

When you begin to create a strategic network, your aim should be to have one person in each of the four quadrants in the Nexus. This will ensure it remains balanced and diverse enough to enable you to achieve any kind of success.

Let's revisit the examples introduced at the beginning of this chapter and put them into their quadrants, as shown in figure 5.2.

Figure 5.2: examples of the Core Four

NETWORK	BUSINESS	SPORT	SEX IN THE CITY	HARRY POTTER
PROMOTER Become more	CEO	Owner	Samantha	Gryffindor
PIT CREW Be more	COO	Captain	Charlotte	Hufflepuff
TEACHER Know more	CIO	Manager	Carrie	Ravenclaw
BUTT-KICKER Do more	CFO	Coach	Miranda	Slytherin

So where do the individuals in your current network sit in the Core Four, and who is missing? To work this out, let's take a look at each of the four in more detail.

1. Promoter

The mind is not a vessel that needs filling, but wood that needs igniting.

Plutarch

A Promoter, or sponsor, is your own personal champion. They are with you, by your side, through thick or thin, never giving up on you, always dreaming big with you. Promoters pull you towards your future dreams, make a noise about potential opportunities, spend time with you to explore how you're going to achieve your goals, and inspire you to become more.

They put fire in your belly and belief in your mind. Their catch-cry is: 'C'mon, let's turn the impossible into the possible ... because you can, I know it.'

Promoters are positive. They cheer you on through the tough times and celebrate the good. They rave about you, make connections for you and open doors. They stretch your thinking to become more than you are or ever thought possible.

Put simply, Promoters believe in you and they want to see you succeed so they tell the world about you.

Your Promoter raves about you even when you're not in the room: 'Hey, have you spoken to Jack? He would be great at that. I reckon you need to pull Jack in on that project. Let me introduce you to Jack—he's an expert in that area.' And if the conversation is not so positive, your promoter still has something to say: 'I'm not sure I'd agree with what you are saying about Jack. Whenever I've worked with him, he has over-delivered and stayed totally committed. I would absolutely welcome him on my team anytime.'

But don't just take my word for it. According to research from the Center for Talent Innovation (a Manhattan-based think tank), people with Promoters (or sponsors) are 23 per cent more likely to move up in their career than those without them. In addition, a 2011 study from the Center for Work-Life Policy published by the *Harvard Business Review* found that active promotion of others can result in a 30 per cent increase in promotions, pay rises and projects for the person being sponsored.

Your Promoter always looks out for you. They invite you to join them at meetings, events and functions. They introduce you to people in their network and encourage you to connect and share value.

I have no doubt that my Promoters are absolutely there for me, and I will be forever grateful for this. They have played a crucial part in everything I have achieved so far, and they continue to cheer me on from the sidelines, encouraging me to do more, be more, live more.

Having a Promoter in your network can completely change the momentum of you, your career and your business. Everyone needs a Promoter. The question is, *who is yours?*

WHO DO YOU KNOW?

- Compare the Promoter checklist against each individual you identified in your network in chapter 4.

- What does this tell you?

- Do you have a Promoter in your network now, or do you desperately need one?

Your Promoter

CHECKLIST

- ☐ cheers you on at all times
- ☐ creates opportunities
- ☐ inspires you to become more
- ☐ helps you explore different paths to success
- ☐ gives you business and career leads
- ☐ is in for the long haul
- ☐ helps you achieve your visions, goals and dreams
- ☐ influences your activity and decision making
- ☐ models behaviour you want to adopt
- ☐ tells you, 'I've got this opportunity for you…'

CHECK-IN

- ☐ Yes, I have a Promoter.

Write in the name from chapter 4: _____

- ☐ No, I need to find a Promoter.

Who do you know who might fit this role? _____

2. Pit Crew

Your Pit Crew keep you true and on track. They nurture you, ensure you are okay at all times and that your emotions aren't getting the better of you. They keep you connected with the present as much as with your future dreams.

Climbing the ladder of success can be a lonely task. Whether you are just starting out, working non-stop in a corporate environment, or pursuing your own entrepreneurial enterprise, the journey requires grit, determination and perseverance. We all experience days of frustration and disappointment, days when we have to face our fears, make tough decisions or calls, push past failures, recalibrate our reality and keep focused on opportunities that lie outside our comfort zone. Having the right crew to help you overcome these difficulties, keeping you mentally tough and balanced, is not just crucial — it's essential.

Captain Joseph Charles Plumb, Jr, aka Charlie Plumb, is a former US Navy fighter pilot and Vietnam POW turned author. He flew 74 successful combat missions over Vietnam, and it wasn't until his 75th flight that his aircraft was shot down. Plumb ejected and parachuted to the ground under fire. He was captured and spent 2103 days as a POW. Years later, he described how he was approached by a stranger in a Kansas City restaurant:

> 'You're Captain Plumb.'
>
> I looked up and I said, 'Yes sir, I'm Captain Plumb.'
>
> He said, 'You flew jet fighters in Vietnam. You were on the aircraft carrier Kitty Hawk. You were shot down. You parachuted into enemy hands and spent six years as a prisoner of war.'
>
> I said, 'How in the world did you know all that?'
>
> He replied, 'Because, I packed your parachute.'[3]

Who has your back? Who packs your proverbial parachute and looks out for you when you make the jump at those critical moments in your personal and professional life?

They may not share the spotlight with you, but they are absolutely riding shotgun alongside you. They go that extra mile, they look out for you mentally, physically and spiritually — because they care about you. They understand your dreams, goals and aspirations, and they encourage you to move forward while at the same time being very aware of where you are right now and what you have to focus on and deliver in the present.

Like a Formula One pit stop, your crew can make or break a race. They fuel your resilience, polish your tough exterior and keep you match-fit for survival and success. When the white flag is waved, you need to dig deep and find the determination to keep going. You need to remain strong and focused on your vision in the face of any challenges or slips along the way.

In her 2007 report 'Grit: Perseverance and Passion for Long-Term Goals', American psychologist Angela Duckworth shares the story of cadets who join the US military academy at West Point and are put through their paces in the Beast Barracks initiative program. This program tests their physical, emotional and mental strength. Surprisingly, Duckworth found that it wasn't strength, smarts or leadership potential that defined success. Rather, it was the individual's grit, perseverance, determination and mental toughness.

In Duckworth's TED talk 'The Key to Success? Grit', she says,

> Grit is passion and perseverance for very long-term goals. Grit is having stamina. Grit is sticking with your future, day-in, day-out. Not just for the week, not just for the month, but for years. And working really hard to make that future a reality. Grit is living life like it's a marathon, not a sprint.

This describes your crew. In a nutshell, they add stamina — the stamina to run the marathon of your dreams, to navigate complexities and recover from setbacks.

Your Pit Crew help you learn from mistakes and keep pushing on anyway. They celebrate your wins, remind you of your achievements and keep it real.

WHO DO YOU KNOW?

- Compare the Pit Crew checklist against each individual you identified as in your network in chapter 4.

- Notice anything?

- Do you have a Pit Crew member in your network now, or do you need to find one?

Your Pit Crew

CHECKLIST

☐ cares about *you* as much as your goals and dreams

☐ connects you to people that matter and makes introductions that count

☐ keeps you balanced so you live in the here and now as much as the future

☐ keeps you match-fit for sustained energy over the long term

☐ ensures you are balancing your career needs with personal needs and caring for the important relationships in your life

☐ encourages you to be more and to embrace who you are

☐ checks in with you regularly

☐ asks, 'How are you?'

CHECK-IN

☐ Yes, I have a Pit Crew member.

Write in name from chapter 4: _____

☐ No, I need to find a Pit Crew member.

Who do you know who might fit this role? _____

3. Teacher

Experience is the only thing that brings knowledge, and the longer you are on earth the more experience you are sure to get.
L. Frank Baum, *The Wonderful Wizard of Oz*

A life of continuous learning is essential to growth. But here's the thing: it's up to you to include in your core network a Teacher who can support you in this way. A Teacher expands your knowledge and pushes you to become better every single day. Successful people know this; that's why they have an insatiable desire and commitment to learn more, in more ways than one.

Many people don't invest in their own mastery. They live a life of stasis, thinking they know all they need to know. Some of them leave school, complete their apprenticeship, get their degree and then stop. They think that's where the learning ends, which couldn't be further from the truth—it's where it really begins! (But you know that. I don't have to convince you because you're reading this book about learning to build the right network.)

Learning doesn't just happen in the classroom. It's not about the letters that come after your name. It's about learning what you do well, how you can do it better and where you can find the Teacher who can help you. Teachers spark inspiration, they instil values, feed curiosity, help you look for answers.

In his book *Rich Dad, Poor Dad*, Robert Kiyosaki talks about his two dads—his 'Poor Dad', who was stuck in a middle-class rut with limiting viewpoints on money, and his 'Rich Dad', who was one of the wealthiest men in Hawaii. Kiyosaki chose to learn about managing money and the money mindset from his 'Rich Dad', which is what he attributes his subsequent success to.

You need to have the right Teacher in your network. The right Teacher and guide stretches your thinking, challenges your ideas and encourages you to push further and keep learning, because they know that this constant curiosity creates real opportunity for growth, achievement and success.

Learning is a self-directed desire and a choice. You must choose to keep learning. You must choose the right Teacher in your network.

Harvard professor Linda Hill says, 'You can't think of something new unless you are being pushed to think in new directions, and you can't do that unless you are engaging with people who have a different viewpoint.'

WHO DO YOU KNOW?

- Compare the Teacher checklist against each individual you identified in your network in chapter 4.
- What can you see?
- How many teachers are in your network now?
- You may have to find one if you don't have one.

Your Teacher

CHECKLIST

☐ shares their knowledge and experience

☐ helps you create the path to success

☐ models behaviour or knowledge you'd like to adopt

☐ discusses your ideas and guides you through your thinking

☐ presents you with information you haven't seen before

☐ possesses more experience than you

☐ challenges your thinking

☐ encourages you to be curious about possibilities

☐ says, 'I've been reading/listening to/watching … and this is what I think. What about you?'

CHECK-IN

☐ Yes, I have a Teacher.

Write in name from chapter 4: _____

☐ No, I need to find a Teacher.

Who do you know who might fit this role? _____

4. Butt-kicker

It is not only what we do, but also what we do not do, for which we are accountable.

Molière

Four years ago I set myself the target to triple the sales in my business, write a book and start a speaking career. Yes, they were lofty goals and I had no real idea how I was going to achieve them, and yes, I was scared. But I didn't just cower in the corner. I got off my butt and recruited a Butt-kicker who would (and did) make sure I delivered.

I was forced off the couch and out of my comfort zone and held accountable for my goals. My first book, *From Me to We*, was published by Wiley in January 2014 and I joined the speaker circuit in August that same year. My sales targets were achieved and my business has grown from strength to strength since. And now here I am the author of a second book, which was beyond my wildest dreams.

That absolutely could not have been possible if I had floundered around on my own in my pyjamas. Having goals and aspirations is one thing; actually accomplishing them is quite another.

We find a million and one excuses not to do what we say we're going to do. We suffer from 'paralysis by analysis'. Or, if you are anything like me, you get attracted by the shiny stuff—a better idea, a more exciting plan—which whisks you off track and zaps your time, energy and focus into the ether. As Lewis Carroll says, 'Any road will get you there, if you don't know where you are going.'

Cue Butt-kicker please!

You need a Butt-kicker to whip you into shape and help keep your eye on the prize. They are your wake-up call, your 'Seriously? Just get on with it'.

Butt-kickers are masters of delivery. They listen to your dreams and accelerate your goals by making sure you stick to them. They hold you accountable for your actions and decisions, and ensure you do what you say you are going to do — and then some. Your Butt-kicker is equivalent to your personal trainer at the gym. They count your push-ups and pull-ups, and they always make you do one extra for good measure.

Linda Galindo, author of *The 85% Solution: How Personal Accountability Guarantees Success*, believes Butt-kickers are our secret weapon to success. 'Working with a partner prevents the ready-fire-aim approach that a lot of entrepreneurs use.'

In a survey of CEOs, the *Harvard Business Review* found that those with formal butt-kicking, mentoring arrangements felt certain their company performance had improved as a result. Most CEOs reported making better decisions (69 per cent) and improving how they fulfilled stakeholder expectations (76 per cent).

It's clear that kicking your butt ensures you avoid procrastination. Butt-kickers help you grow through guidance, mentoring, setting goals and ensuring you deliver on your commitments.

Many people wrongly assume that their Butt-kicker is their boss (or their mum). Sure, your boss may drive you to manage your workload, personal development and career, or even to clean up your desk. Sometimes they may also feel like an unwelcome monkey on your back. But your boss is not your Butt-kicker unless they're encouraging you along the path towards your future goals. A true Butt-kicker has your back — they're not riding on it.

Take, for example, this book. It simply would not have happened without a Butt-kicker. I had a goal, sure, and a clear message I wanted to share. My publisher set the deadline, yes, but that deadline would not have been reached if I had not engaged my own personal Butt-kicker — my editor (thanks, Kelly!) — who held me accountable for that delivery date. I needed to be pushed, motivated and held responsible for weekly phone calls and actions. I had honest and truthful feedback on the content at every step, and advice on how to craft it to be clear, concise and compelling.

The result? You're reading it right now.

WHO DO YOU KNOW?

- Compare the Butt-kicker checklist against each individual you identified in your network in chapter 4.

- Who is kicking your butt for you?

- Do you have a Butt-kicker you can call on when you need to?

Your Butt-kicker

CHECKLIST

☐ asks you about your goals and plans and how you are going to get there

☐ checks in on your progress regularly

☐ expects clear deliverables

☐ gives you honest feedback: the good, the bad and the ugly, flagged for improvements

☐ keeps you focused and decisive

☐ holds you accountable

☐ helps you navigate challenges and find new solutions

☐ helps you do more with less

☐ says, 'You can do it, just get on with it.'

CHECK-IN

☐ Yes, I have a Butt-kicker.

Write in name from chapter 4: _____

☐ No, I need to find a Butt-kicker.

Who do you know who might fit this role? _____

What did you discover?

The idea of this exercise is to look at your list in chapter 4 and allocate each individual in your network to one of the four personality types.

Did you find you already have a Promoter? What about a Pit Crew, Teacher or Butt-kicker? More importantly, who is currently missing from your network?

When I run this exercise with clients and at workshops, most people discover that they have only two of the quadrants covered. In fact, I don't think I've ever had anyone declare confidently that they had all four ticked off.

Most of your connections now probably fall into your Pit Crew and one of the other Core Four categories. It's likely you have a lot of personal connections in your network at the moment, which is why you'll usually find at least one Pit Crew member.

This exercise raises a lot of questions for people. You'll probably find yourself thinking things like:

- *I don't have anyone I can rely on for XYZ.*
- *I don't have anyone to kick my butt.*
- *Should I be looking outside of my industry?*
- *Is it wrong for me to feel like I think differently from everyone else around me?*
- *I don't have anyone I look up to.*
- *I've got lots of friends but no-one who really does XYZ.*
- *I could put so and so in this quadrant, but they could fit into this quadrant as well.*
- *Is it okay to assign one person to two roles?*

These are all great questions and observations! They mean you're really starting to analyse and think carefully, strategically even, about your network.

Now you're starting to think about the support you need, you may also begin to question yourself, perhaps feeling like you are being selfish or self-centred because you don't feel like you have the right support around you.

Clarifying the purpose of your relationships is absolutely not selfish. I'm not asking you to drop any friends or family, but rather to assess the mutual value of your relationships.

This also means being decisive and picking one quadrant for one person, even if you feel like that person could fill two roles. Time is precious for everyone, so get clear, get focused and decide on one role per person.

You will also find that particular people play different roles at different times in your life. That is why assessing and reassessing your network is a constantly evolving process. For example, my Butt-kicker from four years ago has now become my Teacher. Your network doesn't just become static once you have built it. It's a living, breathing thing that will continue to change as you and your needs and goals change.

You must own your own network and be strategic about its growth — that's the only thing that stays the same.

How to find your Core Four

So, your first priority will be to find people in your network who fill all four roles. To do this, you'll need to get clear on what you're looking for and why. What are your current goals and aspirations? Who can help you achieve them? Who do you need to help promote you, teach you, support you or just plain kick your butt?

Is there anyone around you who could fill the gap if you connected with them and asked? Think about people you trust, people you know from LinkedIn, who live outside your department, your company, even your industry.

Are there individuals who inspire you from afar? Start following them online, reading their stuff and absorbing their work before you attempt to connect with them.

Often finding the people who are missing from your network really is as simple as thinking about who you know and then connecting with them to see if they can help you in some way.

This is not about connecting and asking people if they can be 'in your network'. Rather, you need to think about what you can offer someone and what value they can offer you in exchange.

We'll explore this in more detail in part III. It's really important you understand this properly before you skip ahead and just start connecting with people you think can help you, *so I'd encourage you to keep reading until you're ready*.

But before you make any attempts to connect, let's expand on your Core Four and meet the 12 key people and personalities who will really accelerate your success.

6

Seek out your 12 key people and personalities

So you've started on the path to building a strategic network that works for you. Finding your Core Four—Promoter, Pit Crew, Teacher and Butt-kicker—is the essential first step. But real momentum towards your goals does not kick in until you expand on your Nexus to incorporate the 12 key people and personalities.

A quality network of 12 will allow you to build your future strategically, leverage opportunities and mutually exchange value, and accelerates you towards inspirational thinking and exponential growth.

Start with four and aim for 12 key people to fast-track your success.

However, who you think is in your network and who you actually have there may be two very different things. For example, you may have included your boss in your network, but their key focus is actually on achieving *their* objectives, not yours.

Do they sit down with you for deep conversations about your career progression and growth? Are they sharing their learnings and inspiring you to do more and take on more? Or are they so busy in their own world that they never have time for you? Do their leadership behaviours and attributes reflect the kind of person you ultimately want to become, or do you roll your eyes at what they are saying and doing?

Remember the old cliché 'what gets measured gets done'. This is what you need to think about when it comes to your network of 12. You need to really dig deep to understand who is really fulfilling what role, and who you are missing.

As Jim Rohn once said, 'Don't join an easy crowd; you won't grow. Go where the expectations and the demands to perform are high.' This is the only way you will keep control and stay in the driving seat of your successful network.

You might also like to identify your 12 key people online using the Nexus diagnostic tool at **janinegarner.com.au/nexus.**

Meet your 12 key people

The following are your 12 key people and personalities, as shown in figure 6.1:

Promoters — help you to become more

1. Cheerleader

2. Explorer

3. Inspirer

Pit Crew — help you to be more

4. Lover

5. Connecter

6. Balancer

Teachers—help you to know more

7. Influencer

8. Professor

9. Architect

Butt-kickers—help you to do more

10. Truth Sayer

11. Accelerator

12. Mentor

Figure 6.1: the Nexus—your 12 key people

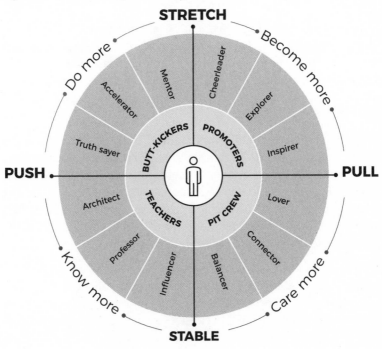

Let's look at each in more detail now.

Promoters

Make noise about potential possibilities and inspire you to dream big, to become more.

1. Cheerleader

Your Cheerleader is exactly that, your number one fan. They rave about you all the time whether you're in or out of the room.

Everyone needs a Cheerleader, pom poms and all. They believe in your dreams, they trust in you and know your capability and capacity, and as a result they jump up and down and make a lot of noise about you. They are your walking billboard, your TV campaign, your social media platform.

When we are children, Cheerleaders are everywhere. They sit in playgrounds sorting out the squabbles, they wait for us at the sack-race finish line even if we are coming in last. They gather in cramped school halls to watch us with encouraging smiles as we deliver a lacklustre musical performance on whatever instrument we have yet to master.

At the 1992 Barcelona Olympic Games, Derek Redmond tore his hamstring in the 400 metres semifinal. His father jumped from the stands, ran to his side and helped his son limp a full lap of the track to finish the race. Redmond was disqualified for being assisted over the finish line. But that race, that moment, will go down in history as an example of the Olympic spirit. And in that moment Redmond's father was his Cheerleader.

Parents are most often our very first Cheerleaders, picking us up when we fall, telling us, 'You can be whatever you want to be.' But when it comes to networking for success today, it's important to look beyond the obvious, because now you need a reality check just as much as unconditional encouragement.

Your Cheerleader is the CEO of your personal cheer club, promoting you whenever they can, sponsoring your growth, creating opportunities for you to shine, pushing you to do more because they believe in you.

They want to see you win. They want to see you succeed.

WHO DO YOU KNOW?

- Compare the Cheerleader checklist against the Promoters in your current network from chapter 5.
- What do you notice?
- Do you have a cheerleader?

Your Cheerleader

CHECKLIST

- ☐ cheers you on at every step of the way
- ☐ talks about you positively to everyone they meet
- ☐ listens intently when you talk
- ☐ provides encouragement even when you're down
- ☐ assists you over the finish line
- ☐ believes in you wholeheartedly
- ☐ pushes you to do more
- ☐ says, 'You're amazing, keep going.'

CHECK-IN

- ☐ Yes, I have a Cheerleader.

Write in name from chapter 5: _____

- ☐ No, I need to find a Cheerleader.

Write down ideas of who you might ask: _____

---

2. Explorer

Real-life adventurer and author Mikael Strandberg defines an explorer as someone who 'is almost always driven by curiosity and a great willpower of making a difference'.[4]

Explorers challenge norms and uncover new paths, so an Explorer in your network will constantly ask you, 'Why?' They want to know what your goals are and how you're thinking of getting there. They are curious about your path to the top and may give you ideas for a different way of accomplishing your feat.

An Explorer isn't interested in what everyone else thinks. They want to know what you think and get excited about the road less travelled and the thoughts less thought. They will force you to remove the lens of normality and replace it with the lens of opportunity. They want you to become more, and they will courageously and fearlessly carve out previously unknown options for you to consider to achieve your ultimate goal.

Curiosity may well have killed the cat, but just as a cat has nine lives, in business, in life and in our career we have to be prepared to reincarnate and open new doors and begin new journeys to get to our destination. The world we are living in is moving so quickly that the only way to remain relevant is also to keep moving, to keep being curious, to keep questioning why you are doing what you are doing. This is the role of the Explorer in our network.

Your Explorer will question why, who, what, where, when and how. They'll disrupt your present situation to introduce you to a new future.

They may encourage you to change your outcome and bring to your consciousness possibilities that previously may have seemed impossibly out of reach.

Successful entrepreneur Nick Holzherr, CEO of whisk.com, describes his Explorer as:

> an entrepreneur, investor and friend who has a significant amount of experience across a broad range of industries and businesses. We bounce ideas off each other, explore options, he shares his insight and this enables me to really look at opportunities and challenges from lots of different angles.

If there is one thing that doesn't need to be questioned, it is this: highly successful individuals do not become that way by idling along in the humdrum car park of life, waiting for progress and profits to come to them.

WHO DO YOU KNOW?

- Compare the Explorer checklist against the Promoters in your current network from chapter 5.
- What do you notice?
- Do you have an Explorer?

Your Explorer

CHECKLIST

☐ exhibits curiosity about what you're doing and why

☐ explores limitless possibilities

☐ shows no fear about doing something different

☐ assists you with challenges

☐ maps out alternative routes

☐ makes you think outside the box

☐ encourages you to think about other options

☐ asks 'Why?' or 'Why not?'

CHECK-IN

☐ Yes, I have an Explorer.

Write in name from chapter 5: _____

☐ No, I need to find an Explorer.

Write down ideas of who you might ask: _____

3. Inspirer

Inspiration is the power of possibility. When you spend time with someone who inspires you, they light a fire within you, they fuel your dreams and energise you to do more, to take on more and become more.

We've all heard the saying 'Enthusiasm is contagious', and it's true. An Inspirer's energy, passion for what they do, courage and self-belief really are infectious.

No matter what you want to do and achieve, having an Inspirer in your network will change everything. They create a picture of a future possibility you can almost see, feel, hear and touch. They inject you with so much enthusiasm and energy that you believe you can take on the world.

The Inspirer awakens you to new possibilities. They transform your belief in your own capacities and capabilities. *Of course you can. Who is telling you you can't? I know you can. If I can, you can!*

In a study conducted by psychologist Marina Milyavskaya[5] students were asked to set three goals that they wanted to achieve by the end of the school semester and to report in, three times every month, on their progress. The study found that those who were more inspired in their daily lives set more inspired goals, which were then more likely to be achieved. The researchers concluded, 'This suggests that goal progress and goal inspiration build on each other to form a cycle of greater goal inspiration and greater goal pursuit.'

This is the role your Inspirer plays. They are ambitious, big-picture, out-of-the-box thinkers who never give in to 'I can't' thinking but instead believe you can accomplish anything you put your mind to.

WHO DO YOU KNOW?

- Compare the Inspirer checklist against the Promoters in your current network from chapter 5.

- What do you notice?

- Do you have an Inspirer?

Your Inspirer

CHECKLIST

☐ expresses passion and enthusiasm freely

☐ fires you up after talking to them

☐ energises you

☐ has big-picture goals

☐ fuels your self-belief

☐ inspires you to see more

☐ makes you believe anything is possible

☐ says, 'Let's take on the world together!'

CHECK-IN

☐ Yes, I have an Inspirer.

Write in name from chapter 5: _____

☐ No, I need to find an Inspirer.

Write down ideas of who you might ask: _____

Pit Crew

Keep you on track, nurture you, prevent untoward emotions from getting the better of you, help you to be more.

4. Lover

Your Lover's primary focus and concern is you and your wellbeing. However, although it's tempting to nominate a significant other in this role, I strongly recommend you don't.

Sure, you'll always have special people there who look after and support you personally, but they don't always need, or want, to listen to everything that's happening in your day-to-day work. This can actually put pressure on our most valued personal relationships.

The other danger is that the people who love us the most will generally tell us what we want to hear, not what we need to hear. Your Lover has to be someone who is 100 per cent honest with you all the time — even when it hurts! Their brutal honesty about your behaviour or the decisions you're making can cut you right to the core. This can often be hard to take from a lover in real life. It's not a personal attack; it's the truth you need to hear.

Of course, you may still feel that a family member, friend or even lover fits this role, and that's fine, especially if they are working with you on your business. But I still recommend that after initial selection of your 12 key people you seek out someone else to fulfil this role.

It's natural for us to put the needs of others — our children, partner or staff, for example — before our own. So our needs get pushed to the back, and we suffer as a result. The Lover in your network doesn't let this happen.

Your Lover puts you and your needs first to help you become the best you can be in times of hardship as well as in times of success.

Singer-songwriter (and ex-cheerleader) Paula Abdul sums up your Lover beautifully: 'Everyone is your best friend when you are successful. Make sure that the people you surround yourself with are also the people that you are not afraid of failing with.'

WHO DO YOU KNOW?

- Compare the Lover checklist against the Pit Crew in your current network from chapter 5.
- What do you notice?
- Do you have a Lover?

Your Lover

CHECKLIST

☐ cares about you first and foremost

☐ gives you honest feedback at all times

☐ remains positive when things are tough

☐ looks out for your wellbeing

☐ values your personal relationships

☐ makes sure you put your needs before others

☐ picks you up when you fall

☐ asks, 'How are you, really?'

CHECK-IN

☐ Yes, I have a Lover.

Write in name from chapter 5: _____

☐ No, I need to find a Lover.

Write down ideas of who you might ask: _____

---

5. Connector

In his best-selling book *The Tipping Point,* Malcolm Gladwell describes Connectors as:

> people who link us up with the world, who bridge Omaha and Sharon, who introduce us to our social circles—these people on whom we rely more heavily than we realize are Connectors, people with a very special gift of bringing people together.

Your Connector opens doors for you, whether to other people or to information.

Sure, you may have a network, but you'll be limited by who you know, your experience and how long you've been at it without a Connector on board.

Connectors have (you guessed it) connections. They are powerful brokers of information and contacts. They have an innate ability to open doors and make connections between people and information, creating opportunities that might have been unheard of previously—and they love doing it!

This is common sense to them. Why wouldn't they introduce you to someone who could help you? There doesn't have to be any reason other than that they see the potential connection so they make the connection. They see first what's in it for you and second, if at all, what's in it for them.

Having a Connector in your network gives you a distinct edge. When they understand your goals and needs, your Connector keeps their eyes and ears open for you. They are always thinking about you, your business, your dreams, your personal and professional strategies, and when the right opportunity presents itself the Connector makes the call, sends the email, talks about you—and the brokering happens.

Your Connector joins the dots you can't see; they know that connecting you to someone or something will create an opportunity for you to fast-track your dreams.

Connectors are brilliant at expanding your network because they can easily pull together information from different networks and make it relevant to you and your goals. Your Connector is absolutely someone you should call on to introduce you to someone you're searching for — such as any of the 12 key people who are missing from your network!

WHO DO YOU KNOW?

- Compare the Connector checklist against the Pit Crew in your current network from chapter 5.
- What do you notice?
- Do you have a Connector?

Your Connector

CHECKLIST

☐ appears to know everyone

☐ connects you to opportunities and people

☐ introduces you before you ask

☐ shares information freely

☐ encourages collaboration with others

☐ expands your network and your thinking

☐ opens doors for you that were once closed

☐ says, 'Let me introduce you to ...'

CHECK-IN

☐ Yes, I have a Connector.

Write in name from chapter 5: _____

☐ No, I need to find a Connector.

Write down ideas of who you might ask: _____

6. Balancer

Your Balancer keeps everything aligned and in check. They force you to attach your own oxygen mask before you see to anyone else's.

The key word for a Balancer is *self-care*. They understand that any kind of success relies on a healthy balance between personal and professional goals.

They understand your family and friends are precious and important to your overall physical and psychological wellness, and as important as an investment in your wellbeing and your career. They believe that success is about doing what you love to do in the way you want to do it, and that a balanced lifestyle is not just possible, it's an absolute must for any kind of success.

We all have a PhD in Juggling. Our lives are a clown-act of 'too many balls in the air' and the often disastrous consequences of this. All it takes is one bad move for all the balls to come crashing down around you. Your Balancer helps you catch the balls before they fall, often before you even know they are falling. They tell you when 'enough is enough' and help you stop, reset and re-evaluate.

As a mum of three children, I know this feeling all too well. When I first started a business, all my kids were under six. The everyday juggle was intense and the hours long. My sleeping time was in freefall, my diet got worse and my (previously slightly obsessive) exercise routine went out the window. I was starting to run on empty. Then my husband's employer went into receivership and our steady income stopped. Our stress levels went through the roof! We had to downsize, move house and sell assets.

If it weren't for my Balancer, Vitality coach and expert Nikki Fogden-Moore, I would have struggled to get back in control. Like Nikki, I believe ultimate success is about getting the balance right. Get this right and you'll become more powerful, both personally and professionally.

As Nikki puts it,

> It's vital to have people within your core team of influencers who truly reflect balance, who create the calm in the storm, who demonstrate a sense of wellbeing both in physical and mental approach. As you build your core team of supporters and those you work with on a close basis, your 'balancer' is that key person who you know will always bring you back to feeling centred, your sense of purpose and remind you to pause and take time for yourself as well as your vision and mission.

This does take work. It does take effort. And like everything you've learned in this book so far, you cannot do it successfully on your own or without being strategic about who you ask for help.

WHO DO YOU KNOW?

- Compare the Balancer checklist against the Pit Crew in your current network from chapter 5.
- What do you notice?
- Do you have a Balancer?

Your Balancer

CHECKLIST

- ☐ checks in with you regularly
- ☐ looks out for your physical and mental health
- ☐ ensures you integrate your personal and professional life
- ☐ leads a healthy lifestyle you'd like to emulate
- ☐ tells you when to stop and pause
- ☐ helps you reset and re-evaluate
- ☐ believes vitality is the key to success
- ☐ asks, 'What are you doing to look after yourself?'

CHECK-IN

- ☐ Yes, I have a Balancer.

Write in name from chapter 5: _____

- ☐ No, I need to find a Balancer.

Write down ideas of who you might ask: _____

Teachers

Help you develop knowledge, wisdom and foresight, to know more.

7. Influencer

'Been there, done that': say hello to your Influencer.

Your Influencer has reached a level of success you aspire to. They enrich your learning experience with their own knowledge. You actively learn from their mistakes, heeding their wisdom and advice.

Learning what your Influencer has done well, and what they would do differently if they had their time again, will give you incredible insights and help you avoid having to reinvent the wheel or learn everything the hard way.

Success is a complex process, but someone who has been there and done that can explain exactly how it is, what to do and how to navigate the journey—from their learned experience. Your influencer is instrumental in helping build your confidence and supporting the pursuit of your passion. They may also open doors for you through their own strategic and smart network, which can jump-start or catapult your career.

At the start of my entrepreneurial journey, I asked a successful female entrepreneur who was 10 years into her journey if I could pick her brains over lunch. I didn't want to take 10 years to learn what she had learned. I wanted to move quickly, to add my thinking to the learnings she shared with me, to achieve my dreams quicker. In the end we met, not just for this one lunch, but regularly over the first 12 months I was in business. There is no doubt in my mind that the learnings and insights she shared enabled me to avoid making some basic mistakes in that first year.

Your Influencer will up the ante, give you focus and aid in your decision making.

Why waste your time and resources reinventing the wheel when you can use others' experience and maximise the return on your investment?

WHO DO YOU KNOW?

- Compare the Influencer checklist against the Teachers in your current network from chapter 5.
- What do you notice?
- Do you have an Influencer?

Your Influencer

CHECKLIST

☐ models a life or experience you respect

☐ has already done the job you want or achieved what you want

☐ shares their know-how so you don't make the same mistakes

☐ provides insight to jump-start or fast-track your career

☐ helps with your decision making

☐ accelerates your success

☐ helps you avoid costly mistakes or wasted time

☐ builds your confidence through sharing their experience

☐ says, 'I did it like this, and this is what I learned...'

CHECK-IN

☐ Yes, I have an Influencer.

Write in name from chapter 5: _____

☐ No, I need to find an Influencer.

Write down ideas of who you might ask: _____

---

8. Professor

Richard Branson once said, 'The day you stop learning is the day you stop living. We should all pick up new skills, ideas, viewpoints, and ways of working every day.' This is how your Professor plays their part.

Your Professor brings fresh ideas, insights and thinking to the table. Maybe they have access to new market data, information and trend reports. Perhaps they're ahead of the curve in terms of what's happening in your industry. In either case, they keep you informed of what's happening now and is likely to happen in the future so your knowledge is always relevant and you are always on top of your game.

Many successful leaders credit a teacher or professor who once helped them at school, university or another point in their life. Our learning should not stop when we leave formal education. Learning new skills and gaining a deeper understanding of your field is essential to your professional success; it's a critical part of any job no matter what the industry or level.

Today's business environment is growing more and more competitive, unstable, fast-paced and demanding, so we have to keep mastering our skill and knowledge to remain relevant. The consumer can have what they want when they want it, with a constant stream of new products, new apps, new concepts and new information, downloadable, deliverable and easily digestible 24/7. Being the best five minutes ago doesn't guarantee that you will remain so five minutes into the future.

Your Professor will, and should, constantly push you to think better, think deeper and think differently.

Learning is not about set-and-forget; rather, it is a continuously evolving process — with a Professor on board.

Conversations with your Professor will never involve small talk; they will be intense, sometimes high level and cerebral. There will be moments when you are so thrilled to have nailed something, but your Professor will push you to take it deeper, to unpack it further. Your role is to accept the challenge of the Professor so you keep growing.

WHO DO YOU KNOW?

- Compare the Professor checklist against the Teachers in your current network from chapter 5.
- What do you notice?
- Do you have a Professor?

Your Professor

CHECKLIST

☐ feels like the smartest in the room

☐ knows the latest books, white papers, TED talks and research

☐ always brings fresh ideas to the table

☐ opens avenues to new data or information

☐ encourages you to keep learning

☐ challenges your thinking

☐ expands your mind

☐ facilitates in-depth conversations

☐ pushes you to dig deeper

☐ helps you uncover new truths

☐ asks, 'What are you reading? What have you learned? What else could that mean?'

CHECK-IN

☐ Yes, I have a Professor.

Write in name from chapter 5: _____

☐ No, I need to find a Professor.

Write down ideas of who you might ask: _____

---

9. Architect

Your Architect helps design, plan and supervise your next steps. They are expert at visualising the consummation of your plans and how to reach that future. They believe all the hard work is in the planning and pre-production stages, and this is where you need to spend a lot of your time.

They are passionate about what you do, are excellent communicators and have fabulous problem-solving skills — all of which are hugely useful to you as you progress through your career or business growth plans. Facing a challenge? No problem, your Architect will work tirelessly and calmly to help you solve it.

Your Architect is methodical, astute and financially savvy, good at identifying potential gains, challenges and risks, and at laying the stepping-stones to guide you along your path.

They'll set milestones and checkpoints, and help you replan at critical stages of your growth.

Just as a movie requires significant investment in the script, approval process and pre-production before moving anywhere near to production, the Architect in your network plays an essential role as the master planner before you move into production. They set specific milestones in the Build of You project, identifying clear checkpoints along the way. They ensure your foundations are solid before you add building block after building block until you get to the *Wow, how did I get here?* place.

Your Architect can help fast-track your success, whether it is writing a book, starting a new venture, negotiating a pay rise, pitching to investors or migrating to another country. Whatever your challenge, they are the Architect of your dreams.

WHO DO YOU KNOW?

- Compare the Architect checklist against the Teachers in your current network from chapter 5.
- What do you notice?
- Do you have an Architect?

Your Architect

CHECKLIST

- ☐ visualises what your future might look like
- ☐ helps you create a plan on how to get there
- ☐ problem solves with you
- ☐ communicates with ease
- ☐ sets milestones and achievements
- ☐ ensures your foundation is solid before you move on to the next step
- ☐ acts systematically and logically
- ☐ asks, 'What do you plan to do?'

CHECK-IN

- ☐ Yes, I have an Architect.

Write in name from chapter 5: _____

- ☐ No, I need to find an Architect.

Write down ideas of who you might ask: _____

Butt-kickers

Accelerate your journey, push you to do more, hold you accountable for your actions, help you do more.

10. Truth Sayer

The Truth Sayer is honest and loyal and will force you to commit to your goals with integrity.

Your Truth Sayer has well-established beliefs and values that clearly drive their behaviour and decision making. They are candid, transparent, authentic and real.

They know that the only judgement that matters is the one you have of yourself. If you don't start leading from within, taking control to acknowledge your values and belief systems and fully owning who you are, you will never be capable of being a better person. As leadership expert John C. Maxwell puts it, 'If you are bigger on the inside than you are on the outside, then over time you will become bigger on the outside.'

Your Truth Sayer is here to kick your butt over your behaviour and the direction you're taking. They will tell you honestly when they agree with you, and be equally honest when they don't agree with you.

The Truth Sayer is your go-to, committed to you, your dreams and your goals. They are trustworthy and a great source of strength, encouraging you to be courageous and less fearful. They are a strong motivator for correct action, wanting you to take responsibility for yourself and your actions, to own all of you, to live it and work it because you are unique.

Your Truth Sayer will challenge your integrity, your honesty and your truth even if this flies in the face of conventional wisdom and the norm.

Are you really being true to yourself? Did you make that decision because you wanted to make it or because you felt like you had to?

Your Truth Sayer will make sure you stand in your own spotlight, shine in your own way, say what you want to say and do what you want to do rather than being dictated to or led by others.

WHO DO YOU KNOW?

- Compare the Truth Sayer checklist against the Butt-kickers in your current network from chapter 5.

- What do you notice?

- Do you have a Truth Sayer?

Your Truth Sayer

CHECKLIST

☐ tells it like it is at all times

☐ gives you honest and critical feedback

☐ challenges convention

☐ ensures you hold yourself to your ethics

☐ makes you courageous

☐ exhibits clear values and beliefs

☐ encourages you to take ownership of your actions

☐ says, 'This is what I really think...'

CHECK-IN

☐ Yes, I have a Truth Sayer.

Write in name from chapter 5: _____

☐ No, I need to find a Truth Sayer.

Write down ideas of who you might ask: _____

---

11. Accelerator

The Accelerator makes things happen and accepts no excuses for inaction.

Most of us think long and hard about what we want to achieve. We think, and we think...and we *think*. We think so hard that we eventually think ourselves out of action. If we're not thinking about it, we're discussing it. We discuss the idea, product or concept until we're blue in the face. Put simply, we discuss it until it's dead.

This is when your Accelerator kicks in. Whether you have a plan, a dream or a project to deliver on, they will kick your butt into action so your idea doesn't remain just that—an idea.

Your Accelerator grabs procrastination by its ankles and hurls it out of the window. They push you and prod you to make decisions, to stick to plans, to do what you said you were going to do.

They make you commit to your goals. They will hold you accountable and will check in on you regularly to see how you're progressing.

They know that if they keep on top of you, you will deliver on the goods and achieve your best results.

They will test you and convince you that even 80 per cent is 'perfect'. They will encourage you to face your fears, to get out of your own way and just do it.

I catch up with my Accelerator via a 30-minute phone call every Monday. We discuss the week that was, what we achieved and any losses, as well as the week ahead — my key focus, sales targets and where we are at with our key deliverables. This commitment keeps me accountable. We are there for each other to drive momentum and progress.

Seth Godin says, 'Surround yourself with people in at least as much of a hurry, at least as inquisitive, at least as focused as you are.' I say, this is where you will find your Accelerator.

WHO DO YOU KNOW?

- Compare the Accelerator checklist against the Butt-kickers in your current network from chapter 5.
- What do you notice?
- Do you have an Accelerator?

Your Accelerator

CHECKLIST

- ☐ kills procrastination
- ☐ makes things happen out of nothing
- ☐ accelerates your progress
- ☐ helps you set key achievables
- ☐ maintains rigour and focus
- ☐ keeps you accountable for your goals
- ☐ drives momentum
- ☐ says, 'Get on and do it!'

CHECK-IN

- ☐ Yes, I have an Accelerator.

Write in name from chapter 5: _____

- ☐ No, I need to find an Accelerator.

Write down ideas of who you might ask: _____

---

12. Mentor

You are never too good to need a Mentor. They provide advice and guidance. A Mentor is empowering and enabling, pure and simple.

Record producer Quincy Jones credits Ray Charles as his Mentor. The empire that is Oprah Winfrey[6] cites the late Maya Angelou as her Mentor. 'She was there for me always, guiding me through some of the most important years of my life. Mentors are important and I don't think anybody makes it in the world without some form of mentorship,' Oprah once said.

Most of the world's most successful and memorable people attribute some of their success to the help of their Mentor. A Mentor will absolutely raise your game.

And don't just take my word for it. A survey of 45 CEOs with formal mentoring agreements (*HBR*, April 2015) found that

71 per cent said they were certain that company performance had improved as a result. In 2014 a survey of 187 businesses[7] found that 70 per cent of small businesses that engaged a Mentor survived for five years or more. For those who worked without Mentors, the success rate was half of that.

Whether in a formal or an informal arrangement, Mentors are crucial to your growth and success. They guide and inspire your career choices, providing wisdom to keep you on track and inspired.

Professor Stacy Blake-Beard, of Simmons College in Boston, believes the best mentoring relationships are found where both similarities and differences exist, where individuals 'share a common ground and learn from alternate perspectives'.

An objective Mentor helps you make intelligent and informed decisions. They will warn you of potential pitfalls and provide a level of protection to keep you out of trouble and enable you to grow. In this way a mentoring relationship can give you an edge. It's why mentoring relies on a high degree of trust.

Mentors may be older and wiser than you. They may have been there before or have experience in the area you need support in. If you are a recent graduate or in the early stages of your career, a Mentor is critical. Often the reality of work and responsibility, and managing the nuances and politics of a career, is very different from the theory learned in a classroom. A good Mentor will help you identify and focus on your strengths and set goals, and will support you as you navigate the complexities of work.

Mary Barra, CEO of General Motors, credits her success to the Mentors she has had throughout her career. As she puts it.

> When building *your* network of mentors, be honest about your mid- and long-term career goals, and how hard you are willing to work to achieve them. Then turn to those who best know you and your work. Earn their respect and trust so they will extend their personal capital to you with confidence and be your professional champion.[8]

John Wooden writes in *Success* (September 2008), 'An individual needs to be open to being mentored. It is our responsibility to be willing to allow our lives and our minds to be touched, moulded and strengthened by the people who surround us.'

WHO DO YOU KNOW?

- Compare the Mentor checklist against the Butt-kickers in your current network from chapter 5.

- What do you notice?

- Do you have a Mentor?

Your Mentor

CHECKLIST

☐ invests their time and energy in you and your success

☐ possesses a certain amount of knowledge in your area

☐ uses their experience to help you

☐ shows characteristics that you admire

☐ plans next steps and actions with you

☐ guides your personal or professional choices

☐ shows an interest in you and your journey

☐ says, 'Let's do this in the next 90 days.'

CHECK-IN

☐ Yes, I have a Mentor.

Write in name from chapter 5: _____

☐ No, I need to find a Mentor.

Write down ideas of who you might ask: _____

Where are you now?

So how was that? What have you discovered? Which of the 12 key people and personalities do you have in your network, and which are you missing?

When I work through this process with my clients, they quickly realise that the network they thought they had isn't anything like the network they need to help them achieve any kind of success.

But don't worry, you're actually in a great position because you now know who you need in your network. It's by identifying these gaps that you become clear about whom you must seek out.

Now you can take control and strategically align yourself with the right people who will fast-track your goals and ambitions.

Remember, your network does not and should not consist solely of people who think like you. To achieve true diversity you need to balance the 12 key people across industries, experience, genders and geographical locations. That may mean rethinking some people who are in your network and trying to find other individuals to broaden your network.

You need one person, and one person only, representing each of the 12 key personality types: one Cheerleader, one Influencer, one Explorer and so on. Only in this way, as Carl Jung's personality typing revealed, can you achieve the right kind of balance.

This probably means you will need to find people to fill certain roles, but it may also mean you have to cut back your network (especially if you listed 15 people in your original list in chapter 4 — you're aiming for 12, remember).

As noted in the previous chapter, it's likely you'll find individuals who could fill more than one role, in which case you'll need to nominate them for just one and find someone else to fill the other.

It's also likely by now that you have identified certain individuals in your network who are actually not supporting you in a way you need. In the next chapter, we'll refine your network further, so you can identify these imposters.

7

Sink the 12 Shadow Archetypes

I once had a boss who was a great connection, on paper — female, successful, results oriented, a great supporter of me and my work. Over time, however, as my success and network of influence grew, her behaviour changed.

Once productive meetings became discussions of negative details; my big ideas, which had once been embraced enthusiastically, were shut down; my personal ambitions were devalued and marginalised. I was clearly and continuously put back in my box. A woman who had once inspired me now began to limit me.

A strategic network is not just about having 12 key people; it's about having the *right* 12 people.

In chapters 5 and 6 you learn to identify your Nexus, which comprises a Core Four among 12 key people. These are the individuals who will positively influence your future, the people who will work collectively to stretch you and push you further than you could ever go alone. These are the right people to have in your network.

Think of your network as your baby. You need to love it, protect it, nurture it, and provide constant care and attention. Parents are always on top of who their children associate with; we absolutely don't want them to get in with the wrong crowd. We need to think of our network in the same way.

With the good comes the bad.

It might seem unlikely that you would associate with someone who doesn't support you or your work, but often their negative impact won't be immediately evident. It is only with time and experience that you begin to recognise the subtle interventions that keep you small, or behaviours that are incongruous with the lifestyle you actually want to lead or the person you want to become.

This may not be easy, but it's up to you to make sure you don't have any negative influences affecting you and your decisions.

I've said that every 12 months I review my network of 12 to make sure I am surrounding myself with people who are going to help me achieve my dreams. At the same time, I am continuously moving on from any negative influences, because I want to surround myself with people who want to grow and live a positive life.

As multimillionaire businessman and philanthropist Tony Robbins puts it, 'Who you spend time with is who you become. Change your life by consciously choosing to surround yourself with people with higher standards!'

Knowing who to cut from your network is as important as knowing who to keep.

Many of us stay stuck in the comfort zone of connecting with the same people all the time, or staying connected with people just because we've known them 'forever'. Many of us tolerate personal and professional connections who drain us of energy, inspiration and momentum.

But now you have the opportunity to question who these negative characters are!

Someone wise once said, 'People come into your life for a reason, a season or a lifetime. When you figure out which one it is, you will know what to do for each person.' And that's exactly what we're going to figure out now.

Success is not selfish

Thinking about who to cut from your network may very well make you feel uncomfortable or even downright self-centred. The idea of putting yourself first (not second, third or even at the bottom of the list), and being strategic about who you choose to ride alongside you on your personal journey to success can make us feel, well, icky.

But remember this: Your network is for *your* growth — not your mum's, your boss's or your neighbour's. Your 12 essential people and personalities, whom you identified in the previous chapter, are there to help you *become more*. This is all about your success and personal achievement, no-one else's. If you want to have any kind of success — and happiness — in life, you need to surround yourself with the right crew.

Surrounding yourself with people who, consciously or unconsciously, work against your growth and achievement is crazy!

Look closely at your network again, and ask yourself if any of the people in it:

- drag you down
- make you doubt your abilities
- never seem to have ideas of their own, but always say yes to yours
- always see the negative in every situation
- put you on the defensive
- make you hesitate about your decisions and what you want to do

- talk about themselves all the time and show little interest in you

- take your ideas and comments for their own?

It's time to own *you*, to own your dreams, goals and ambitions. It's time to own not just what it is you want to become but also who you want to be. It's time to own your today and your tomorrow—personally and professionally.

I'm not asking you to cull your Facebook friends or to tell your aunty why you can never see her again. And I'm not recommending you tell whoever it is 'You're fired from my network!' This is about figuring out who you want in your inner circle and who is not supporting you or your journey, but you don't have to literally tell them!

Once you identify the negative people in your life who limit your progress, then you have the choice as to how much time, if any, you give them. You can put up boundaries, manage your time and manage their impact on your energy. Only then can you really start to shine and accelerate your success. The 12 key people in your network are a collective power, as we discussed in chapter 3.

Deepak Chopra puts it like this: 'Negative people deplete your energy. Surround yourself with love and nourishment and do not allow the creation of negativity in your environment.'

Who is working against you?

The purpose of building a strategic network of 12 is that it works for you and not against you. Lurking in the background, however, are 12 characters—or Shadow Archetypes—who will limit your potential and obstruct your goals and success (figure 7.1):

Burners—want you to become less

1. Saboteur

2. Back-stabber

3. Dream Stealer

Underminers—want you to care less

4. Traitor

5. Narcissist

6. Energy Vampire

Judgers—want you to know less

7. Sceptic

8. Labeller

9. Villain

Fighters—want you to do less

10. Bully

11. Liar

12. Critic

Let's look at each closely now.

Figure 7.1: the 12 Shadow Archetypes

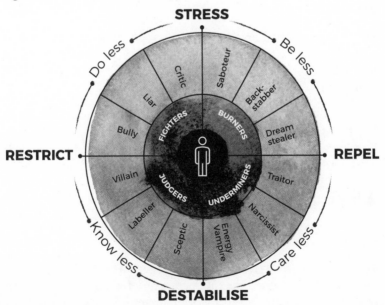

Burners

As hard as it may be to accept, there are people out there who don't really want you to succeed. They may just want you to stay exactly who you are, as you are. These Burners are usually scaremongers who are frightened that you will leave them behind or achieve more. They'd rather you stuck with the status quo and didn't become 'too big for your boots'. Sometimes there's a strategy behind this (maybe they see you as competition); at other times they may not even realise they are sabotaging your success.

1. Saboteur

The Saboteur sets out to destroy or damage your success deliberately and usually for personal gain. Sometimes they may even take your idea and run with it. They enjoy asking lots of questions, spending one-on-one time with you so they can pick your brain, and likely use that knowledge for their own end game.

While imitation is said to be the sincerest form of flattery, many of us find this a bitter pill to swallow.

Perhaps you've had an idea, made a suggestion in a meeting or among friends, even developed a new product or service offering, and then found your Saboteur spruiking it as though it was their own.

When you are determining the direction of your career or business, working hard every day and innovating tirelessly to bring new ideas to fruition, watching someone piggyback on your work and talent can be devastating. That's if you allow it to be.

2. Back-stabber

The Back-stabber is someone you usually think of as a friend — until they stab you in the back.

The Sydney Morning Herald (24 September 2014) cited a LinkedIn poll in which more than 50 per cent of under-24s admitted they would happily betray a workmate to get ahead. In the same article, a senior psychologist at VOICE Psychologists and Allied Professionals in Brisbane reported hearing of:

> a health professional being berated by a supervisor for the poor quality of her reports, who later found out that the same supervisor was later putting her own name to those reports and passing them up the line as if they were hers.

It happens; I've witnessed it many times over the past few years. Colleagues and clients have shared their disappointment, hurt and frustration after someone copied their jewellery designs or marketing idea or even blog posts that were sold to a media outlet as their own.

3. Dream Stealer

A Dream Stealer sucks up all your positivity, inspiration and self-belief. They are usually spotted hanging out around the water cooler or lurking in the office kitchen. They can be friends, colleagues, even family members, who genuinely seem to want to protect you. You may think they have your best interests at heart, but subtly they'll fill your mind with doubts about your dreams and ambitions.

They rarely add constructive ideas to your vision, likely because they don't—and don't want to—understand the journey you are on. Instead of providing support and encouragement, their commentary feeds your inner critic with negative self-talk to persuade you that what you're doing won't work.

Underminers

Remember back to your school days and that one friend who seemed absolutely wonderful but was actually undermining you behind your back? Unfortunately, this adolescent mindset is prevalent in the grown-up world too.

Underminers zap your positive energy and make you feel like you constantly have to defend yourself or justify your behaviour. They don't support your career or personal goals because they are too focused on themselves and where they fit into the picture. The only place for an Underminer is in the playground.

4. Traitor

Know someone who says one thing but does something else — usually something that comes at a cost to you?

In today's world, collaborative thinking is the key to success, but some people — the Traitor, for example — still don't get it and view the world only as a competition. 'This is my dance space — and if you step on my toes, I will step back. Harder.'

Maybe you have shared secrets or ideas with them, and they have then revealed those to someone else. Or perhaps one minute they appear to be your fiercest and most loyal supporter, backing you all the way, and the next they are doing and saying the complete opposite. Disloyalty like this undermines your self-esteem and confidence. Put bluntly, it's two-faced.

5. Narcissist

The Narcissist is interested in one thing only: maintaining their own power. They have an exaggerated sense of self-importance, take more than they give and believe they have the solution to everything. They do not like to be challenged on this. They lack empathy, guilt or remorse.

These narcissistic tendencies undermine you and erode your confidence. Your conversations likely end up as debates or arguments. Everything they say or do centres on what they want and need, boosts their own ego and implies others are inferior.

In an interview for the *Australian Women's Weekly* (30 September 2016), Julie Hart, head psychologist and director at The Hart Centre, observes, 'There's a huge level of degrees from one extreme to the other but I would say, probably, up to about 15 per cent of the population have some degree of narcissism in them.' *Eek!*

6. Energy Vampire

The Energy Vampire, aka Negative Neville or Debbie Downer, has nothing positive to say, ever. They constantly blame others and make excuses for their situation instead of taking ownership of their own behaviours and actions.

In their report 'Managing Yourself: A smarter way to network' (*HBR*, July 2011), Rob Cross and Robert J. Thomas suggest that energy-zapping interactions have seven times more impact on you than energising ones, and that 90 per cent of anxiety at work is created by just 5 per cent of a person's network. In your network of 12, that is usually down to your Energy Vampire!

Spending time with this person zaps your purpose and passion, drains you of momentum and leaves you feeling down in the dumps and grey with the world. And if you're achieving while they are not? They have an excuse for that too: 'Well, you've got the time / the contacts / the thousands of followers / the money / the pit crew / the experience / the resources ... whereas I don't.'

Judgers

Ever feel like someone is constantly judging you and all you do? This group of offenders also breeds negativity, judging not just you but everyone else in your network. They judge your goals and ambitions, as well as your achievements and successes. This creates barriers to your growth, knowledge, insight and intellect, serving no purpose except to feed doubt and insecurity, and to block your progress.

7. Sceptic

The Sceptic wants to bring you down (likely with them) before you achieve too much. They believe your ideas have no merit, feed off your inner fears, and wreak havoc on your anxiety and stress levels. They are there on the sidelines watching and waiting, and they love it when they can say I told you so.

To make matters worse, it's our minds and bodies that bear the brunt of it. Our self-belief takes a battering, and the self-criticism and negative self-talk kicks in and paralyses us.

Accepting the Sceptic's opinion of you and any of your ideas is giving them value they don't deserve.

8. Labeller

The Labeller puts you in a box with a neat little name on it and sets your limitations: 'You are too junior.' 'You've never worked in this area before.' 'You're a busy mother—you can't possibly do [XYZ].' And they will only support and appreciate you if you fit into this box or the label they have created for you; anything else and you'll be 'disappointing' them.

Imagine if Do Won Chang[9] had listened to the people who placed him in the box of Korean immigrant and low-paid worker when he first arrived in the US in 1981. In those early days he worked three jobs to support his family, as a janitor, in a gas station and in a coffee shop. In 1984 he pushed himself out of the box and opened his first clothing store. Now Forever 21, a multinational, 480-store empire that is still family owned, generates around US$3 billion in sales a year.

9. Villain

The Villain in your network is malicious in intent, motivated by power, greed and jealousy. They appear to set up conflict, obstacles and challenges for you and the people you hang out with.

Their toxic personalities and mean-spirited activities can increase your stress, raise your blood pressure and affect your performance. They make it difficult for you to get work done. They can act in a sneaky way, enjoy gossiping and often use their manipulative tactics against you.

But as Winston Churchill said, 'You have enemies? Good—that means you've stood for something in life.' In this case it means you're on to something—you're on to your success.

Fighters

Fighters do just that: they fight you every step of the way along your road to success. They hold you back with the intention of bringing you down with them. They can't bear to see you achieving when they are not. 'How dare you have your own ambitions and aspirations! How dare you demonstrate focus, integrity, drive and determination! Keep that junk out of your head and stick with me in the status quo.'

10. Bully

A Bully fights you from all angles, breaking down your spirit until you feel like you have no hope left. Often they appear in the guise of a friendly competitor, until they start intimidating and even humiliating you.

They can make you feel submissive, small and without a voice. They exclude you from conversations, meetings or events. They may even become abusive (verbally or physically).

Bullying, in whatever form, is a serious issue around the world, from the playground to the boardroom. In a 2011 Monster Global Poll survey [10], 64 per cent of the 16 517 participants admitted to being bullied at work. According to the Australian Productivity Commission, workplace bullying costs Australia between $6 billion and $36 billion annually.

11. Liar

Who isn't telling you the truth? Who is lying intentionally for their own gain? Liars deliberately hold back important information from you, and I don't mean the answer to 'Does my bum look big in this?'

Maybe they offer to help with your project, but never deliver. Or suggest an introduction to someone who could help you land a new job, only you're never connected. They may even put you forward for a role or a job, or so you think, but then nothing ever eventuates, no matter how much you follow up.

There's always an excuse, and when they've run out of excuses there's usually silence. This leads to frustration and disappointment. The Liar's 'carrot dangling' can impact your business deals, stunt your career growth and ruin your relationships as well as your own personal brand.

12. Critic

The Critic shuts down your goals, plans, ideas, thoughts and actions before they've even begun. They criticise your plans, fill your head with negative nonsense and opinions that lack evidence or substance.

They have strong ideas about what success means, how to live life, do business or build a career, and they're not interested if you don't think or feel the same way. It's either their way or the highway.

It doesn't matter how strong you think you are, the Critic's constant stream of negative commentary will eventually wear away at you until you're no longer a 'worthy' opponent.

WHO DO YOU KNOW?

- What have you discovered from this introduction to the 12 Shadow Archetypes?

- How many Burners, Underminers, Judgers or Fighters do you have either in your network or dangerously close to you?

- Revisit and reassess who is in your network now.

- Do any of the 12 key people and personalities from chapter 6 exhibit characteristics of the Shadow Archetypes?

- Do you need to break with them and find other people to fill the key roles that will help you fast-track your success?

12 Shadow Archetype checklist

BURNERS

☐ Saboteur

☐ Back-stabber

☐ Dream Stealer

Underminers

☐ Traitor

☐ Narcissist

☐ Energy Vampire

Judgers

☐ Sceptic

☐ Labeller

☐ Villain

FIGHTERS

☐ Bully

☐ Liar

☐ Critic

Work your network

Being aware of the impact others can have on you is powerful, because with this knowledge and awareness comes choice.

Will you choose to take ownership of and control of the key people in your network? As I've said, it's not about telling your best friend why he or she cannot be in your network; it's about defining and recognising boundaries and identifying those people who will help you get to where you want to be.

Choose to play your own game in the way you want.

Choose to live the life you want.

Choose to take control of your own energy, mindset and momentum.

Choose to make your network work for you.

Mark Twain said, 'Keep away from people who try to belittle your ambitions. Small people always do that, but the really great make you feel that you, too, can become great.'

Be brave and reassess the negative people in your network, and instead find a diverse network of Promoters, Pit Crew, Teachers and Butt-kickers who will add value to your thinking, your business and your ambitions. These are the people who want to help and support you, to guide you on your personal journey, ensuring you are moving forward in the right direction, the direction you want to head in.

All you need now are the tools to 'work it', to master the art of building your effective and strategic network. This is what we'll get into in part III.

PART III
HOW

So there you have it. Now you know the secret to success: your 12 key people and personalities.

Your Promoters, Pit Crew, Teachers and Butt-kickers will push and pull you towards your goals, stretch and challenge you, encourage you to reach out beyond the status quo, help you achieve what you never thought possible.

Hopefully your network already includes individuals who fill many of the roles you identified in chapters 5 and 6. But it's highly likely that working through part II has identified gaps and some real 'aha' insights into who you need to find to make up your network puzzle of you.

Do you need to cut from your network someone who functions as one of the 12 Shadow Archetypes? Do you need to find a Cheerleader, Professor, Mentor or Balancer?

In the next part, we'll explore how to go about filling these gaps. We'll explore the tools you need to start to really work your strategic and smart network.

Coasting through networking events and virtual connections will not transport you from here to success. In fact, it will risk undoing all the great work we've done!

So you must be very clear on your own personality, what your goals are, what you're searching for and why, and then make sure your interactions are consistent and purposeful.

You need to work through three key stages:

1. CHOOSE—What are your goals and why are you networking? Chapter 8 will help you uncover your own personality so you can work out how to make networking work for you.

2. CONNECT—How do you connect in the right way? Find out in chapter 9.

3. CULTIVATE—What value can you offer others? Chapter 10 reveals the secrets to networking like a real pro.

Let's see how.

Choose who, what and why

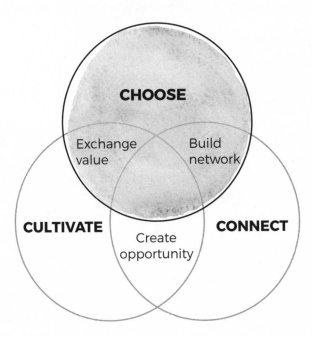

CHOOSE

Exchange value

Build network

CULTIVATE

Create opportunity

CONNECT

In the classic movie *The Wizard of Oz*, Dorothy, a quiet country girl, and her best friend Toto the dog are transported by a tornado from their home in Kansas to the Land of Oz. Their dream, their goal in the story, is simply to return home, so they 'follow the yellow brick road' to the Emerald City to find the wizard who can make any wish come true.

Along the way they meet the Scarecrow, who believes everything would be perfect 'if only he had a brain', the Tin Man, who wants a heart, and the Cowardly Lion, who thinks life would be sorted if he only had courage.

When our band of adventurers (note that with Dorothy, they form their Core Four) finally arrives at the Emerald City after fighting off the Wicked Witch of the West, they are grateful to be granted a meeting with the wizard. Until, that is, they discover that he is in no way magical, but merely a wise old man. Still, the fake wizard delivers on his promise, if not in the way they had expected: he gives the Scarecrow a diploma, the Tin Man a heart-shaped ticking clock, the Lion a medal for courage, and Dorothy a chance to fly home in his hot-air balloon.

So what's the point of sharing this story?

As we make our way along our personal yellow brick road, our own journey, we constantly make excuses for what we lack. 'If only' is the catch-cry that holds us back from our dreams. Actually we already have the answers for what we seek within us. It's simply a matter of choosing to accept who we are — our strengths and our weaknesses, our good and bad bits. That is the answer.

As author Marianne Williamson puts it:

> Our deepest fear is not that we are inadequate. Our deepest fear is that we are powerful beyond measure ... Your playing small does not serve the world ... and as we let our own light shine, we unconsciously give others permission to do the same.

Developing clarity on who you are, what you're looking for from your network and what you can provide in return is as essential for effective networking as it is for the advancement of your career and personal development. To connect with the right people and build a network that works, you first need to:

- establish your goals and dreams so you can make the right decisions and meet the right people to take you there

- understand your values so you can consistently walk your talk

- identify your strengths so you can share them

- own your weaknesses so you can seek help on them

- be yourself so you are authentic and true.

You need to own your vision of you and what it is you want to achieve in your career and life.

Say yes to goals that ensure forward momentum, and say yes to owning who you are and who you want to be.

Own yourself and your goals

When it comes to building an effective network you must be clear on what your goals and aspirations are, how others can help you achieve them and how you can help them in return.

It's worth considering which of the 12 key people you could be for each of those in your network. What do you offer others? You'll often find you are different things to different people at different times. So reassessing this as often as you reassess your own network is crucial.

You need to ask yourself:

- *What skills and strengths am I bringing to the conversation?*

- *What weaknesses do I have?*

- *What am I passionate about?*

- *What problems can I solve for people?*

- *Why do I want to network?*

- *What is the vision I ultimately have for myself?*

- *What do I want to achieve right now?*

- *What help and support do I need to achieve my goals?*

- *Which of the 12 key people and personality types do I think could be me now, and for whom?*

Your dream and vision for yourself and for your business and career is yours and yours alone to own. So you have to believe in yourself, first and foremost. Getting clarity on your personal brand — the who, what and why you are doing what you are doing — will enable you to build a network that works for you. It will give you the confidence to network with conviction and, most importantly, increase your ability to exchange value that matters.

Owning yourself is about learning to share your strengths and skills to help others out while at the same time acknowledging your weaknesses and accepting help. It's about accepting who it is that you are, warts and all, and being brave enough to consistently walk your talk. You need to accept yourself and all your imperfections, learn to rise above your limitations and refuse to let negative thoughts control you. This is about working on and managing your mindset and self-belief.

When I was first transitioning from my secure corporate job into the unknown territory of an entrepreneurial life it was scary. I had three young children, a wonderfully supportive husband, a well-thought-through plan and a dream. To manage my mindset and build my self-belief, I wrote down four mantras that I repeated to myself every morning and night:

1. 'I am successful.'

2. 'I can do everything I want to do.'

3. 'I am knowledgeable about what I know.'

4. 'I can do this; I am in control.'

These days I still talk to myself like a champion with power and personal conviction. If you don't believe in yourself first, how can you persuade others to believe in you?

When we own who we are, the most natural conversation and viewpoints flow. Hierarchy or position in a company should not matter or dictate your approach. Whether you're at a meeting, a conference or a networking event, being true to yourself will create impact, as your behaviour is a natural extension of who you are.

Own what you're doing and why

In his book *Outliers*, author Malcolm Gladwell proposed that it takes 10 000 hours of practice to achieve mastery in a field. Among the examples he cites are:

- Bill Gates, who used to sneak out of his parents' house at night to go and code at his Seattle high school

- The Beatles, who went to Hamburg five times between 1960 and 1962 and performed a total of 270 nights in just over a year and half. When they finally arrived in the US in 1964, their first burst of success, they had performed live an estimated 1200 times! Most bands don't do that in their lifetime.

It doesn't matter if you agree or disagree with Gladwell's theory; the point is that every one of us is an expert at something because, whether we realise it or not, we have built up time and hours practising. Yet we undervalue our experience and ideas because we don't believe in ourselves; we feel like imposters, we don't think we've clocked up enough hours.

You have an equivalent of 10 000 hours in something, whether you realise it or not. This is what makes you unique. This is what you can stretch and develop further, share with others and use to create new opportunities.

Ask yourself: *What is my area of expertise? Am I owning it?*

Start standing for something. Start being known for something. Start speaking up and sharing your value and your dreams and what it is you are looking for. You might be a digital marketing expert, a wordsmith, a philanthropist with a big purpose, an expert at branding who is looking to connect, collaborate and contribute to building mutual success. You might be a skilled graduate looking for a job or a CEO looking for a board position or seeking help to navigate the complexities of global expansion.

When you are known for knowing something, your ability to cut through the crowd and get noticed increases exponentially.

More than 20 years ago Jeff Bezos, the CEO of Amazon, saw something no-one else could see. He has since turned Amazon into the world's second most admired company (after Apple), and, despite his reputation for being highly demanding, thousands are drawn to his vision and aspire to work for him.

Bono, the lead singer of U2, uses his rock star positioning and mass appeal to influence and drive worldwide change. His influence helped persuade global leaders to write off debt owed by the poorest countries. Through his ONE and (RED) campaigns, he enlists organisations and millions of people to combat AIDS, poverty and preventable diseases.

Since beginning to work with the UN's refugee agency as a goodwill ambassador in 2001, Angelina Jolie has undertaken 50 field missions to countries in crisis, including Iraq, Syria and Pakistan. Her decision to explain her pre-emptive double mastectomy in a *New York Times* editorial created much controversy and further illustrated her willingness to take a public stand and start the difficult conversation. Former UK foreign secretary William Hague said of her, 'Angelina Jolie represents a new type of leadership in the 21st century. Her strength lies in the fact that she is able to influence governments and move public opinion at the same time.'

The reality is this. You matter. Every choice and action you take, every word you speak, has the capacity to influence others and, in turn, the decisions being made at that moment in time. Your views are unique to you. There is nothing wrong with making your own profile as strong as you possibly can. Don't be afraid to be brilliant. Have the resilience to shine and follow your dreams. Walk the talk, own your skills, strengths and goals, commit to the change you want to see and build a network of people around you who want to see you succeed.

Your network is your responsibility, not your organisation's.

Sure, you may have a fantastic organisation that is willing to invest in you and your networking skills; however, the key point here is that you are also networking for your own personal and professional growth and development, not just to the benefit of your organisation's.

Where *they* see value may not be where your value is. You must learn to stand on your own two feet, and often you'll need to make that stand away from the crowd. Sometimes this may also mean that you have to decide to make a financial investment. I witness too many corporate employees who would love to join certain networks but decide that unless their company pays for it it's a no-go. That is crazy logic!

Building a network that works for you and your personal and professional growth matters. This fundamentally is an investment in your future.

But ... I'm an introvert

I've lost count of how many times I'm told, 'I can't network, I hate it, I'm just an introvert.' To this I say: 'Rubbish! That's an excuse you're using to keep you at the ineffective stage of the networking ladder.' (See figure 2.1 in chapter 2.)

Whether you are an introvert or an extrovert, you can still network—you just need to do so in a way that works for you.

Introversion and extroversion are at the heart of human nature, yet depending on our comfort zone we unconsciously make judgements and place ourselves and one another into boxes. Extroverts may see introverts as unsociable and standoffish. Introverts may see extroverts as aggressive, egotistical and socially needy.

Who's to say who is right and who is wrong? As co-founder of Quiet Revolution Susan Cain says, 'The secret to life is to put yourself in the right lighting. For some it's a Broadway spotlight, for others a lamp-lit desk.'

The Swiss psychiatrist and psychotherapist Carl Jung believed, 'There is no such thing as a pure introvert or extrovert. Such a person would be in a lunatic asylum.' And yet many of us continue to label ourselves, and judge others, as occupying one or other extreme of the spectrum.

We have to embrace our inner introvert or extrovert, and learn to accept and respect the natural disposition of others and ourselves.

Embrace who you are

When it comes to networking, if you feel like you are introverted then embrace your calm, measured and thoughtful approach, your ability to develop ideas independently and with reflection. Know it's absolutely okay to want to be on your own, to turn down an invitation to an event, and high-five yourself, with confidence, that you are a proud non-sufferer of FOMO. Own the value you bring to thinking, debate, conversation and idea generation.

If, when networking, you enjoy the energy you get from socialising with many, from connecting and communicating with friends and strangers alike, then embrace your natural, assertive nature and 'let's-go-get-em' attitude. Bring the fun and keep being the high-energy extrovert you are, because we love the fact that you are able to bring people and groups together.

In both cases you bring significant value to networking situations.

An introvert will generally:

- think before they talk
- engage in deep conversation

- focus one on one
- be thoughtful in their follow-up.

An extrovert will generally:

- jump right in, introducing themselves to everyone
- engage in light banter
- socialise with many
- find follow-up fun.

And it's perfectly okay to fall somewhere in the middle, able to adapt and morph depending on what the situation requires. In either case, there is no excuse not to network!

When you embrace who you are and your natural style, you start to enact change. Margaret Thatcher's extrovert personality helped her battle her way through cultural barriers such as a deep-rooted British sexism to become the country's first female prime minister. Winston Churchill's limitless energy helped him lead the British people through World War II, while he wrote prolifically throughout his life, winning the Nobel Prize in Literature for his body of work.

Famous introverts have also changed the world. Gandhi changed the direction of an entire nation. Warren Buffett, considered to be one of the most successful investors in the world, has pledged to give away 99 per cent of his wealth to philanthropic causes. Bill Gates is generally more comfortable with technology than people. Darwin is celebrated for his inner curiosity, Dr Seuss for his inner imagination.

Become more aware of how to work to your strengths in a networking situation and make it easier on yourself, because when you spend too much time battling your own nature you deplete your energy and focus and ultimately your goals become harder to achieve. On the flip side, when you make life choices that are congruent with your temperament, you unleash vast stores of energy.

Too many people live lives that don't suit them — introverts with frenetic social schedules, attending large networking events with thousands of people; extroverts with jobs that require them to sit in front of their computer for many hours at a stretch with no opportunity to socialise. We all have to do things that don't come naturally some of the time, but it shouldn't be all the time. It shouldn't even be most of the time.

Get out of your own way

Seek congruence with your natural style, own it and stop faking it till you make it. Get out of your own way, get out of the box you have put yourself in and embrace who you are. Only then will you network in the right way.

There is an iconic scene in the movie *Pretty Woman* in which a character says, 'Welcome to Hollywood! What's your dream?' So many of us have a dream, a plan for our future; a vision of what we would like our lives, careers or businesses to be. We may even understand our key driver, or, as leadership expert Simon Sinek expresses it, our 'why' — *why* we want what we want.

The real question, however, is how much do you actually want your 'why'?

What excites you? What fuels the momentum that carries you from initial idea to making it happen? What pushes you out of a place of procrastination and 'maybes' into a space where you seek the right people to add to your network and advance your career? How hungry are you really?

Many of us get lost in planning rather than doing. Somewhere along the way we forget we *have* to take action or we become frozen in '*oh but...*' lists. Worse, something doesn't quite go to plan and we fall back into our comfort zone because it's way too scary to step outside.

Anyone who knows me understands I am an advocate of creating a vision and a plan with focused goals to deliver over 90 days. This book is all about having a plan — a planned approach to building a network of you.

The difference between reading this book and implementing it is actually all down to you. It's ultimately up to you to get out of your own way, to decide that you want to change what you are doing right now, to take control of your network and to drive your future success.

Fear less

Being clear on who you are, what you're doing and why you're doing it is one thing, but actually getting out there and building a network of transformational connections that matter — well, that's another. Fear can be debilitating, even crippling. It can stop you achieving your dreams, stop you from challenging the status quo, from using your voice, from trying something new.

To get out there and connect, to build your network of 12 key people, you have to be brave. You have to believe in yourself, and fear less.

We all experience fear and loss at some stage in our career — loss of face, loss of market share, loss of revenue. We question ourselves: Can I?' 'Who would want to listen to me?' 'Do I have the experience to do this? These are the crazy thoughts, the irrational fears we sometimes feel when we're trying something new or unfamiliar. But fear is a choice.

You can choose to be paralysed into inaction or you can choose to turn fear into a powerful tool for success.

Fear less about conforming and doing what everyone else wants you to do—going to university, getting that job, getting married, buying a house, having kids, getting promoted. This is not the only definition of success. It's more important than ever to own your vision and your own dreams, to lead yourself and be the leader you want to be.

Fear less about standing in your spotlight and shining, about having an opinion. Speak up. Yes, people may disagree, argue with you even, but what someone else says about you is not your concern. Don't compare yourself to others, because what *you* believe and say matters. Stand solidly in the space of you and remember that differences of opinion drive change.

Fear less about promoting yourself. Don't be afraid to emphasise your strengths, what you add in terms of value and, most importantly, your point of difference. In an authentic, realistic way, tell the world what makes you unique. Use what sets you apart as an effective marketing tool.

Fear less about not having all the answers, about not always being right and about having to ask for help. Embrace a life of constant curiosity, of questioning, of learning from your teachers, from each other, from people around you every day. Find your 12 key people to support your growth, because together you will be smarter and stronger.

John C. Maxwell asks, 'Will you sit at the top of the hill merely contemplating your capabilities? Or will you give yourself a little shove and barrel down that hill, knocking over obstacles in your way?' This is your choice. And in the next chapter you'll see it's how you make that choice to connect with others that matters.

Download the CHOOSE worksheet to help you get clear on who you are, what you want and why: **janinegarner.com.au/resources.**

Choose wisely and frequently

At the age of 40, Paula thought she had met everyone in her life she would ever need to meet. But when she became CFO and acting CEO at the world's largest provider of flexible workplaces, Regus Australia, Paula says she felt 'like I was standing on top of an iceberg—isolated, with no-one to ask for help'.

She realised that what she had thought was an effective network actually wasn't supporting her at all. She needed to seek out people who were at the same level as her or above her; she had to expose herself to those facing the same problems she faced.

Paula needed a personal board of advisers around her, an intelligence bank, a marketing machine. She needed Promoters, Teachers, Butt-kickers and a Pit Crew who would help her deliver her goals, stretch her thinking and challenge her to do more.

'Little did I know at the time that building a network was an ongoing exercise to ensure my personal and professional strategic goals aligned to the people I was around,' Paula says. 'As my goals changed, my network had to change too.'

Like Paula, you need to evolve and grow your network in line with your personality and your professional and personal goals. And you have to understand that, although it requires much thought, time and energy, this investment will benefit you on your journey tenfold in the long term.

'A strong network is mission critical if you are concerned about your future,' Paula adds. 'Invest the time to work out who, what and why. Find the influencers, advisers and advocates who will help you grow and the team that will keep you balanced and grounded. Networks build networks. You cannot afford not to do this.'

Connect in the right way

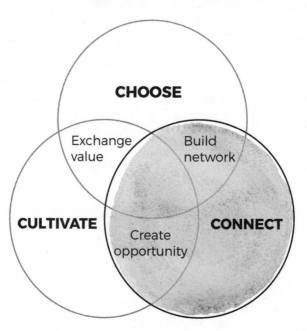

At a recent client meeting, Craig, a senior executive, shared with me that he had decided to take redundancy from his organisation after almost 13 years of service. He was excited at the opportunity to take some time out to reconnect with his family and refuel his energy. His plan?

'I'll start looking for work again in about six months, I reckon,' he said.

'Who do you have in your network who can help you?' I asked. 'Have you thought about what you're going to do between now and then to keep your profile out there?'

'Oh, I haven't really thought about that, to be honest,' he responded.

What do you think about that strategy? It's not an unusual response, especially when we're a bit tired and need a break. But nurturing your network is an ongoing process. It is not something you switch on when you want something and switch off when it's not needed.

In his book *What Got You Here Won't Get You There*, Marshall Goldsmith discusses 20 bad habits that stifle success, such as making excuses and passing judgement. He then explains how these habits stand between your current and your next level of achievement. Well, I'm going to add to this list, and say number 21 is sitting on your hands and doing nothing until the time is right.

When we forget to invest the time or energy in managing or nurturing our important relationships, we get lazy, do nothing and let our networks evolve organically. The result? Remember the ineffective, transactional stage of the networking ladder in chapter 2?

After all your hard work, rethinking and assessing your network, and searching out the 12 key people who can accelerate your success, why on earth would you let all that go to waste?

It is up to you to make the decision and choose to connect, engage and nurture the people who matter to you on an ongoing basis. Only in this way can you build a network that will be influential and transformative for you over the long term, including at stages in your career or life when you feel you want to 'take a break'.

An ever-evolving process

As shown in part II, successful networking is about understanding the connections you should be making—the 12 key people—as opposed to those you *are* making. It's about managing those networks and connections and adding value to them at all times.

In his book *Highly Effective Networking*, Orville Pearson suggests that while building a large network can give you an edge, the more pivotal factor is learning to maximise and leverage existing contacts.

Your network is a living thing that has to evolve as you grow and evolve.

You move jobs, you get a promotion, you move countries, you have a baby—at every step of the way your network has to morph to match your changing circumstances.

You must ensure you are constantly surrounded by a circle of key people who will stretch you, challenge your thinking and hold you accountable for your decisions. Investing the time to review your network regularly is essential.

For me, this is something I do every December/January as part of my new year goal setting and planning. As well as creating my vision board for the year and my key goals in the area of business, finance, personal and relationships and checking in on alignment with my bigger-picture why, I also review my network of 12.

Do I still have the right people around me? Is there still a mutual value exchange happening? Have they or I moved on in terms of key goals and focus? What's missing and who do I need to connect or reconnect with? What help do I need in the next 12 months to achieve my goals?

As Craig's story at the beginning of this chapter illustrates, building a network that works is about taking ownership and ensuring that at all times you surround yourself with the people who matter to you. It's also about appreciating that cultivating transformational connections requires an investment in your time, energy and focus.

Assess your network regularly—do the exercise in chapter 4 and download the Nexus online to identify your network of 12 at key points in your career: **janinegarner.com.au/resources.**

Closer than you think

Building a strong personal network doesn't just happen. You have to put in the time, energy and commitment to bring your ideal network to life. You have to put into place the plan you came up with in part II, when you identified your 12 key people. It's now about finding the missing connections and making contact.

The good news is that your successful network is probably closer than you think. Small degrees of separation exist between you and your next opportunity, so take some time to explore those closest to you and the people you already know.

There are three actions you need to take to connect with the right network:

1. Reach out.
2. Hang out.
3. Link in.

These actions do not work independently of one another but rather work in unison. So let's look at each in a bit more detail.

1. Reach out

You already have a network of sorts at your fingertips. Your friends, family and work colleagues are all connected to a wider world beyond your own personal network. Most of us have heard of the idea of *six degrees of separation*, which proposes that anyone on the planet can be connected to any other person through a chain of acquaintances that has no more than five intermediaries.

There is no doubt in my mind that only small degrees of separation exist between who you already know and who you could potentially know—you simply need to ask. Each person in your existing network should be able to suggest one other person who might be of interest to you and make an introduction based on what you need.

Don't undo all your good work! Think strategically about who you want to connect with and figure out if anyone else you know could help make an introduction.

Think about who has currently achieved what you want to achieve or shows the behaviours you want to exemplify. Take the time to work through the 12 key people properly, review the checklists, and identify who is missing and who could help you get to where you want to go.

What skills are missing? What insight do I need? What attributes and behaviours am I seeking? How can I spend more time with that person? What would they be interested in reading? What do I have that they might be interested in? Where do they hang out? Who do I already know who might be able to introduce me?

The other day I was having lunch with a female friend who said she was looking for a Mentor—someone who had already arrived at where she planned to take her businesses next, someone with experience of the challenges and the pitfalls who would be willing to guide her through the next stage of her entrepreneurial journey. I immediately made an introduction to an ideal connection and they are now working together. Two leading businesswomen are now connected and working collaboratively in a mentoring relationship to drive each other's success.

In the early days of my own career I knew I needed to find someone who could fast-track my transition from a corporate salaried position to an entrepreneurial space that was commercially viable and smart. I explored who was already doing what I wanted to do — people who were building practices and selling their thought leadership and expertise — and asked them to recommend who I should meet. As a result of one of these conversations, my mentor and now Thought Leaders business partner became Matt Church.

It really is that easy. Own it. Be curious. Be brave. Reach out — and don't forget to expect the unexpected. Open your eyes to what is out there, because it comes in many different guises.

As Mario Jayaprabhu, a participant in one of my 'Take the Lead' workshops, explains, you need to take the plunge:

> Before the course, I'd consider myself a 'speak when spoken to' kind of networker. But then I went diving in Thailand.
>
> My dive instructor had such diverse talents: a musician, a photographer and a senior executive at a leading investment firm in the US, not to mention being an avid diver.
>
> The more similar someone is to you, the more comfortable it feels to connect, which is why networks are by nature homogeneous. But I realised that James was someone who would be great as one of my 12 key people, and the best thing I could offer him in return was the chance to explore some dive spots in Australia.
>
> So I connected with him and now I'm on my way to clocking the hours to becoming a solo diver as well. Most people concentrate on networking up — building rapport with someone higher than them or around the same position as them on the ladder. But it's just as smart to 'network down' and connect with savvy junior people in your industry or others who might be taking a different path.

2. Hang out

There are endless places, events and networking groups where you can connect offline — the challenge is deciding which one is right for you, your goals, and your personality and style so you don't fall down the transactional rabbit hole.

Once you know who you are seeking, you can start to explore the events where these people gather and therefore where you might meet them. If you are looking for a mentor in the legal space, go to an industry-specific event; if you are a graduate just starting out, then attending a more generic networking event might be more useful; if you are looking to grow your business or career to the next level, then make sure to attend an event with the right calibre of attendees from whom you can gain insight and knowledge. And if you are an introvert, why not think about inviting someone for a coffee or organising a lunch for four rather than facing 400 new faces at a big event?

The key is to be clear on who and what you need, be curious and explore what's out there, and make a decision based on what works and what doesn't work for you. Don't follow the crowd. Remember, this is your journey and your network.

Be willing to step out of your comfort zone. Dig deep and step out of the place of familiarity and safety to connect with people outside your traditional circle of influence. Make a decision to explore other networks, other people, other industries and businesses.

You could try:

- attending events that attract different groups of people
- talking to someone from a different industry
- debating with people of different seniority and from different departments
- engaging with others because you are curious about where that connection might lead.

I've heard of one company starting a monthly game of coffee roulette where all employees' names, irrespective of hierarchy, are placed in the equivalent of a hat and pairs are randomly drawn to have coffee together that month. What a fabulous way of encouraging connection within businesses across seniority, department and functionality!

I see too many people who flit from one networking event or group to another, gaining nothing but a diary packed full of dates and yet another notch on the 'events attended' board. While you may find some inspiration along the way, you'll also end up with a lot of useless business cards.

Remember, while networking matters for business growth and lead generation, this is all about building your network, a network that works for you. It's about networking the right way, about being strategic and transformational.

3. Link in

LinkedIn is a great tool for business lead generation and maximising the reach of your business message, but it's also one of the most important tools at our disposal when it comes to sourcing connections.

Today, LinkedIn has a global network of over 200 million users, and while it gives you the opportunity to share your expertise, your strengths and what you know via your own profile, it also opens connecting doors that were previously closed.

Just as you ask friends, family and existing contacts to make introductions in real life, you can do the same in LinkedIn. But — and this is a big but — just as in real life you have to connect on LinkedIn through a two-way conversation.

Remember, this is not about transacting, it's about transforming your network.

If you've got this far in the book you'll know that connection is not simply about hitting the 'let's connect' button. You have to engage fully, to converse, to share value, and sometimes even connect over a coffee.

Through LinkedIn you can search, find and connect with past work colleagues, university friends or people you met at last week's networking event, or even search globally based on industry, job title and key word. LinkedIn helps you expand your network by offering crucial connections and expertise. Don't underestimate the power of this tool, and remember the first rule of networking: it needs to be a two-way conversation.

If you're looking for more insight on how to make LinkedIn work for you in the right way to transform your network, then you might like to check out branding and LinkedIn expert Jane Anderson (www.janeanderson.com).

Respect everyone's time

When you start connecting and building your network make sure you are respectful of everyone's time — this is the key to exchanging value. Calling someone and asking if you can 'pick their brains over coffee' is not connecting. Neither is calling people and asking them to be part of your network. And sending a LinkedIn request or email with a lot of questions — well, that is actually an abuse of their time.

Get clear on what help you need and be specific in your request. I guarantee most people will be willing to help and if they can't they are very likely to respond with an explanation. As opposed to 'Can I meet you for a coffee?' (which is a sure-fire sign that you're going to chew up their precious time), why not get more specific with, say, 'I'd like to chat with you about the three key things you did to grow your career to becoming a partner' or 'I'm looking to expand into China and noticed you had managed to do so successfully. I'd really appreciate it if you could share your three key insights.'

When meeting people for the first time, be present. Listen to what they are saying, engage in conversation, and ask questions. Take notes, gather intelligence, be diligent, commit to taking action and make sure to say thank you. I realise this is common sense, but you would not believe how many people seem to forget basic etiquette.

Make sure to continue the conversation. Follow up with a thank you and state the action you will be taking immediately. Maybe include a link to a relevant article or white paper that is aligned to your discussion. A few weeks later reconnect and provide an update on the action taken and the results. This shows respect and appreciation for the time they have shared, as well as your commitment and interest in any lessons learned.

The point is you are taking the lead. You led to the original conversation, which was the catalyst for opportunity and opened the possibility of forming a longer-term relationship.

Download sample email templates to connect with people you don't know but would like to know: **janinegarner.com.au/resources.**

Set an example

There is no doubt that building a powerful *web of you* increases your positioning and ability to influence more. With this comes a significant level of personal responsibility and accountability.

It is up to you to:

- be an example to others in your network
- model the behaviour you seek in return
- give knowledge unconditionally
- open doors willingly
- share insight to drive continued growth and success for others
- hold yourself accountable for your actions
- follow up your connections.

Choosing to connect with the people that matter to you will absolutely create opportunity for growth. As Alison Flemming, General Manager Finance Operations, Scentre Group, explains,

> My network helps me appreciate my role and what my organisation does; it enables me to bring fresh ideas into my organisation. Knowing a diverse group of people helps bring in diversity of thought to training programs, development sessions and personal coaching, and it helps me think differently so I'm able to add an alternate or fresh perspective to a lot of business discussions internally.

This is the key to value exchange, which is the subject we explore in the final chapter.

Connect and respect

Building a network is about seeking out best practice. I find people who have a similar mindset and value system and who I can relate to. Trust is essential.

There is a huge amount of learning when you network with people you respect. They tell you honestly what they think, their feedback develops and enhances my thinking, and as a result I become better as a leader and as a person.

I have been very deliberate in building my network. When I have identified a gap I've found someone I respect and emailed them to connect. Most people want to help.

Usually I start with one specific need or question and then the conversation naturally expands. It's about respecting the other person's time, being clear with one question at a time and always providing value back.

People can offer different things at different times, and maintaining relationships takes energy and commitment. But this close network, for me, is priceless. The key is balancing the talking and discussion with decision making and getting on with it.

First impressions are critical. I find that people with the best network are always present. They are on form at all times, friendly, well-dressed; they hold themselves well, add value to conversations, make others feel amazing and are genuinely interested and engaged in the conversation. They are present when they turn up—always. This is something I have seen, watched and learned from and try to emulate in the way I network to support others.

Nick Holzherr, CEO of Whisk.com, an online grocery supermarket that serves many of the UK's largest retailers.

Cultivate connections and exchange value

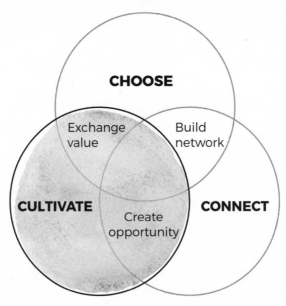

143

I was working with a client, Anthony. We were due to have one of our monthly mentoring meetings but there had been a mistake in our diaries — Anthony was in the city waiting for a face-to-face meeting while I was sitting in my office in the Northern Beaches of Sydney waiting for a virtual hangout. Yikes!

Only the previous week I had introduced Anthony to one of my 12 key people, my Cheerleader, Kieran. As our mentoring session was about to kick off, he bumped into Kieran.

'Hi Kieran,' said Anthony. 'I'm on my way to meet Janine.'

'Great,' said Kieran. 'I'll come up and surprise her.'

At this point, I called Anthony and we discovered the mistake. But then the magic happened.

'Why don't I stay and do the mentoring session?' offered Kieran. 'I've got an hour to spare.'

Win–win. Anthony ended up having us both in on the conversation — one face to face and one on the phone. As Anthony put it, 'I don't think I know anyone who would step in like that for me.'

So who has your back? Who in your network would step in for you?

This is a great example of the power of connection. And this is the network you are aiming for. You know when you've got it down pat: when you've cultivated the right relationships, this mutual value exchange happens organically and naturally.

Networking is a shared experience. It is based on an exchange of mutual value.

A couple of years ago, someone else in my network was diagnosed with breast cancer and needed emergency surgery. During one of our conversations, she shared that she had some client commitments and training programs that she needed to run. They were new clients and she didn't want to let them down.

'Don't worry. Leave it with me,' I said. 'I'll find someone to fill in for you.'

I rang around my Nexus and found two of my 12 key people to step in and cover the sessions. Just because they could and they cared.

This is the type of relationship you need to cultivate with your network.

Now you're clear on why you're networking and how to approach connections with the right intention, you need to make sure you offer value in exchange.

Cultivating your relationships takes you to the tipping point between networking that is mildly effective and networking that works exponentially. When you network with conviction, sure of who you are and what you know, willingly sharing information and insights that matter to others, the following happens:

- Opportunities are created.
- Value is exchanged.
- Influence is increased.
- Connections become transformational.

So when it comes to cultivating your connections, the question to ask yourself is who are you really and what are you really giving? Are you bringing your full self to the conversation or hiding parts of yourself? Are you entering into a conversation with a genuine interest in who you are meeting and what you can do for them? What are you offering in exchange?

There are 10 secrets to cultivating your connections for successful networking:

1. First impressions count.
2. Confidence matters.
3. Speak up to be heard.
4. Listen to be present.
5. Become an action taker.
6. Exchange value.
7. Identify yourself.

8. Be memorable.

9. Follow your energy.

10. Keep your network alive.

Let's take a look at each one in more detail.

1. First impressions count

From when I started school, I distinctly remember my parents drilling into me the importance of making the right first impression. Shoes were always shined, hair brushed, clothes ironed and nails clean. Now, as a parent, I do the same with my children.

The importance of a making the right first impression cannot be overestimated, because first impressions influence later impressions. James Uleman, a professor of psychology at New York University and researcher on impression management, explains: 'You don't get a second chance to make a first impression. In spite of the congeniality of many professional gatherings, judgments are being made and impressions formed all the time.' He adds, 'The impression you create may affect future job opportunities, collaborations or other important matters.'

In his book *Blink*, Malcolm Gladwell suggests that our first impressions usually are fairly accurate and stand the test of time. 'It is a central part of what it means to be human,' Gladwell writes.

> We thin-slice whenever we meet a new person or have to make sense of something quickly or encounter a novel situation. We thin-slice because we have to, and we come to rely on that ability because there are lots of situations where careful attention to the details of a very thin slice, even for no more than a second or two, can tell us an awful lot.

So what's the first impression your network has of you?

Professional? Intelligent? Ambitious? Lazy? Sloppy? Disinterested?

Whether we like it or not, appearance is our first filter — whether in person or online. Everything on the outside contributes to others' initial impression of you. So make it a good one. My mum would say, 'Polish your shoes, dress appropriately, iron your shirt, press your pants ... ' Take control, because first impressions matter.

2. Confidence matters

I have a confession to make: I am a fan of the reality TV show *The Voice*. I love following the contestants' journey from their first audition to the wow moment of 'where have you been hiding that talent'. We see them shine as they progress through each round, gaining in confidence as they perform, their dreams getting closer and closer to that end goal. The stories of self-belief, determination and resilience are inspiring, and the energy is infectious.

This journey hinges on confidence. And confidence *is* infectious. If, as a shop owner or app creator, you could sell confidence over the counter then it would make you millions.

Think about the number of times you have been in a restaurant or a meeting or a presentation, and *that* person walks in. The one who effortlessly grabs everyone's attention. They aren't necessarily trying to capture anyone's glance, yet they look as though they are moving with their own personal cheerleading squad and everyone wants a piece of their attention — including you.

Call it an aura, call it presence. In my mind it boils down to one thing: confidence. The confidence of knowing who you are, what you want and where you are going in life, in your career or in your business direction. The confidence to think, walk and talk with positivity and self-belief.

Confidence is about understanding yourself inside and out. What's your purpose? Your passion? It's knowing your talk, walking it and then being willing to share that with others from a place of generosity and authenticity.

Being confident is also acknowledging when you don't know something, showing your softer and more vulnerable side, and being willing to say, 'I have no idea what's happening here' or 'I don't know what to do here'.

But there are ways of giving our confidence a workout, and the more we work it the stronger our confidence levels will become. In 'Use It or Lose It: The Science Behind Self-Confidence' (*Forbes*, 26 February 2015), Margie Warrell says, 'The good news is that new research into neural plasticity reveals that we can literally rewire our brains in ways that affect our thoughts and behavior at any age.'

She goes on to share the following tips to rewiring your courage:

- Act as if you already possess the confidence you aspire to.

- Find your power pose. (For more on this check out Amy Cuddy's TED talk 'Your body language shapes who you are'—it's brilliant!)

- Channel your heroes.

- Focus on what you want.

- Mentally rehearse and visualise success.

At the end of the day, you are the one who decides whether you are good enough. Nobody else. Self-confidence is essential if you want to become the best you can be and to connect with the right people in the right way. You can either be your own worst enemy or your own biggest cheerleader.

3. Speak up to be heard

How many times have you heard someone say, 'Oh, but I didn't have a choice—nobody would have listened to me anyway'? So they simply went along with the flow in the boardroom, the small-talk chatter over networking drinks or the heated debate at the pointy end of a transaction?

How many times have you thought this yourself when it came to a big decision? *I didn't really have a choice.*

The truth is, we all have a choice. We can own our expertise, and share it openly with others, from a place of wanting to add value and to engage. Or we can sit comfortably silent, keeping our knowledge and insight to ourselves, waiting to be asked.

Worst of all, we can get frozen in the no-man's-land of no self-confidence. *Why would anyone be interested in what I have to say?*

Your opinion does matter. Your thoughts, insights and knowledge matter. You have a voice—use it.

You matter because when you own your voice and speak up, you become an integral part of driving change. Change is vital for you yourself and for others you are connecting and building a network with. Networking, after all, must be a two-way street, an exchange of information between two people, and if you don't speak up then you've chosen to take the one-way street to nowhere.

Your personal success is there to be created if you speak up willingly, openly and with honest and full disclosure. Too often people sit back and say nothing when something needs to be said. They may have an idea that contradicts mass opinion, or an insight that will add to group understanding, but instead of speaking up they remain silent.

If you don't speak out, you are not showing willingness to have courageous conversations with your network. You are avoiding the opportunity to contribute what matters to the collaborative experience. You are not creating the space to gift your knowledge, thoughts, opinions or expertise to others. You are not enabling an opportunity for others to listen, learn and add value to your thoughts. You are not sharing the insight and information that matter to your circle of influence.

In the words of Vera Nazarian, author of *The Duke in His Castle,* 'Yawns are not the only infectious things out there besides germs. Giggles can spread from person to person. So can blushing. But maybe the most powerful infectious thing is the act of speaking the truth.'

Use your voice. Be an engaged part of your network. Change your game and speak up!

4. Listen to be present

Multitasking is seen as an art form these days with communication merely an exchange of information. True connection, the meeting of minds, and the mastery of networking, of actually being present not just in body but also in attentiveness, means switching off from multitasking. Listening is twice as important when it comes to networking.

When you are engaged in conversation are you truly listening or are you rubbernecking, checking out who else is in the room or what other people are doing? Are you focusing on the conversation at hand or listening with one ear, with the other on another conversation? Are you actually there in body but thinking about other things — the to-do list you left at the office, that email you must send later, what you are going to have for dinner? Or are you so in your own head that you are focused on thinking about what you are going to say next?

Building a network that works for you is about connection. Listening is an essential part of connection. And listening plus connection creates understanding and opportunity.

Sean Kim, founder of the Growth List, emphasises this distinction: 'The truth is, most of us are hearing to respond, when we should be listening to understand.'

Effective listening is a skill that underpins all positive human connections. It's easy to get distracted when you are in a room with many others, but you must make a point of staying focused and present. It's about listening and watching for all the verbal and non-verbal clues. Make eye contact, concentrate and make a conscious decision to remove all distractions.

Show a genuine interest. It does not have to be, and actually should not be, always about you. When someone else is talking, really listen to them and resist the temptation to butt in. Just stop and listen. When they have finished talking, then it's your turn.

Listening builds trust. And when you really listen, people feel the connection; they sense the genuine interest you have in them and as a result they often become more open and more honest, sharing more information.

Listen to what people are really saying. Ask questions. Be curious about those around you and explore what is really going on. Take a moment to be interested, to check in. Get to know people — to *really* know them.

Only when we open our eyes and truly look can we see opportunity; only when we open our ears and truly listen can we hear opportunity; only when we open our minds and engage do we 'see' others as they really are.

That is connection. That is networking.

5. Become an action taker

If you say you're going to do something, you must follow through and do it. That is a golden rule of networking that is absolutely non-negotiable when it comes to your own network of 12. When you have spent time with someone, engaging in conversation and exchanging value, then you must make sure your words align with your actions.

This is especially important with your 12 key people. Your ability to nurture your network, to leverage conversations, to constantly give back and deliver, will build the relationship over time. It's about building trust, belief and integrity.

The most important part of managing and nurturing your network is what you do after each meeting or connection. Following up sends the message that you are serious about the relationship, that you are proactive, respectful and willing to invest the time and the effort.

Irrespective of whether it's the first time you've met, a new contact you would like to nurture, or it's someone who is already part of your network, make sure to send them a thank you. This can be via email or you could go old school and send a handwritten note (something I love doing) or even make a phone call (I know, right!).

Thank them for their time, acknowledge what you found interesting about the conversation and consider what, if anything, you can send them that relates to what was discussed. This could be a white paper, an article of interest or the link to a TED talk, for example. If you have committed to an action, add this to your note to confirm that you have listened, heard, understood and are acting on it — that you can be depended on. It doesn't have to be long or formal — you are simply acknowledging the connection and conveying your appreciation of the time spent.

Make sure to connect with them on LinkedIn. Add them to your database, making a note of where you met them, what you talked about and any interesting snippets of information that you garnered.

Successful management of your network requires 100 per cent delivery on what you say you are going to do and any promises you made. Equally it requires you to take on board other people's suggestions — it is disrespectful to ignore them.

Did you offer to make an introduction? Did you commit to deliver an action item? Did you agree to send a sample of something you have been working on? Whatever you agreed to, make sure to follow up. Make the introduction, do the work and then send an update with the outcome.

Make sure to schedule a follow-up — this could be weekly, monthly or quarterly. It's important that you don't just connect when you want something. Connection, deep connection, is built over time. It's about building trust and belief. It's about giving and adding value to them and their lives first, and trusting that this investment will pay off in the development of more transformational connections.

6. Exchange value

Hopefully, by now you've realised that networking isn't about what you can get from someone else; it's about what you can offer in exchange. What do you know? Who do you know?

When you learn to share openly with others with no expectation of anything in return, then everyone benefits. This is the principle of value exchange — giving and taking information, products or services freely to benefit both parties. It's the two-way street of powerful networking.

Value exchange requires trust, faith and the ability to truly engage in conversation, to be switched on to the needs of others and to be curious about how you can help.

The question 'What can I do to help you?' should be running on continuous rotation. And guess what? At the start of any relationship, more often than not you have to give more, making deposits for the future value of the connection.

Value exchange, the cross-fertilisation of intelligence and sharing of skills and knowledge, is the new currency. Collective thinking and active sharing of knowledge and ideas create new opportunities for all. No money changes hands. Each party involved gains knowledge, information and yes, eventually, perhaps even financial reward from their involvement, but the priority is the sharing of information, the connection that is made and the network that is built. The use of skills and thought as currency is something that is only going to increase in a future where knowledge means money.

We all have something to share and something to give. It could be job opportunities, business leads, a white paper, information to help fast-track decisions, a go-to-market opportunity — and of course an introduction between two parties, knowing that opportunities can be found within that connection.

What can you trade? What information do you have to share with your network? Offer to help. Be willing to help. Make connections that matter, share information that matters and foster a pay-it-forward relationship. Show your network that giving is as good as getting.

7. Identify yourself

We have spent a lot of time in this book talking about the 12 key people you need in your network, but which of those people do you think *you* are? Which of the 12 personality types do you relate to? Are you often sharing information with others, making connections or kicking people's butts?

As we touched on in the previous chapter, you will play different roles for different people at different times in their life. You may be a Mentor for one, a Cheerleader for another and a Balancer for others. It's normal to wear multiple hats.

It probably won't surprise you to learn that I am naturally a networker and a Connector. I am always suggesting introductions between people and brokering information for mutual benefit. I often see connections before others have made them, and I usually whip out my smartphone and make an introduction there and then. Instant follow-up. Absolute action taker. But while I am a Connector for some, I know that I also play the role of Inspirer, Mentor or Teacher for others.

Knowing the role you play, or at least being curious about it and asking others in your network how you might help and what value you can add to them, is how you continue to pay forward in the cycle of value exchange.

Think about what value you are offering to others.

8. Be memorable

I was having lunch with a very good friend of mine and we were discussing innovation and thinking outside the box.

'The challenge, Janine,' she said, 'is that too many people are generic.'

And you know what? She is right. There is too much sameness and beigeness going on, with people doing and saying exactly what's expected, obsessed with keeping small talk the norm rather than engaging in interesting, insightful, sometimes maybe controversial conversation.

Conformity is not memorable and is not the key to success. Differentiation is. Matt Church, the founder of Thought Leaders Global, believes it's all about 'becoming known for knowing something'.

Have the courage to own what is unique about you, what it is that you stand for, what problems you can solve, and above all keep investing in the mastery of your skill.

Become memorable by working your quirks, because we notice things that are different, unique, out of the ordinary. My good friend Dr Jason Fox is memorable not only for his thought leadership but also for his red hair and beard, his quirky sense of dress and mannerisms, just as Seth Godin is memorable for his bald head and glasses.

With so much information at our fingertips there is no excuse not to feed your personal intelligence bank continuously, whether through the latest news online or an inspirational TED talk or white paper. There is no excuse for being bland and boring.

In *The Compound Effect*, Darren Hardy discusses the concept of garbage in, garbage out. 'If you want your brain to perform at its peak you've got to be more vigilant about what you feed it,' he says. Feeding our brains with mind-numbing sitcoms or reality TV shows is simply garbage in, he suggests:

> all that drive time radio yak...drives your thinking process, which drives your expectations, which drives your creative output. That IS bad news. But just like a dirty glass, if you flush it with clean water...long enough, eventually you will end up with a glass of pure, clear water.

Hardy suggests that instead of garbage we should be feeding our brains strategies of success, inspirational stories, ideas for growth. This is what makes you interesting and memorable — the information you have, the ideas you share, the stories at your fingertips.

I have my own personal junk and inspiration filter. I watch very little TV, don't read newspapers or listen to the news. I have very select feeds so I can keep track of relevant news, I subscribe to some key publications that improve my knowledge, I treat myself to a coffee date every week when I either read a book abstract or watch a TED talk and I read — a lot!

So ask yourself what is influencing you? How are you feeding your 'interesting and being memorable' bank?

9. Follow your energy

Sometimes you will feel de-energised and wish you were somewhere else — this is one of the biggest killers of conversation and connection. You aren't engaged or present so why should anyone be interested in talking to you?

It's important to understand where you get your energy from, where you can be your best and perform at your maximum capacity (whether you are an introvert or extrovert, as discussed in chapter 8).

As an extrovert you'll love the larger networking events where there is lots going on. You are inspired by the collective energy of the crowd and the noise, which will leave you feeling pumped and ready to take on the world. As an introvert you are more likely to be energised in small-group settings in a quieter location where you can engage in deeper, more thoughtful conversation.

There is no right or wrong. Or rather, the only wrong is constantly forcing yourself or being forced to do something you don't enjoy. Sure, sometimes we may just have to suck it up, but not all the time. If you feel drained and on edge, then no value can come from it. Work out what works for you and follow that — not someone else's program. Respect your natural disposition.

If you enjoy what you do you will be more energised and this will shine through. You will be more present and therefore get more value out of it. You have to love what you do to have a sense of being and a mission to achieve. When you have this, work becomes fun and you remain connected to what is going on around you.

If you are passionate about what you do, you will have unlimited energy and this in itself becomes contagious; you will naturally attract like-minded thinkers. 'As you tap in to your inner networker,' says Devora Zack, 'others will start gravitating towards you.'

10. Keep your network alive

Nurture your network and seek out opportunities to add value all the time.

Take the lead and expect nothing in return. If you continue to give in this way, then I promise you it will come back to you, in spades. You will boost your personal positioning and your reputation, and you will be seen as someone who is committed and invested in building relationships that matter.

You have the ability to influence one to one, many to many, more to more. Your team, your colleagues, your leaders, your children, their friends, your friends, your family; but true influence requires one critical thing: you must be you, be interested, be invested.

Regular communication drives this. Once again, don't just connect with the people that matter in your network when you want something. Take time to think about the key people in your network. What support could they do with right now? What are they working on that you might be able to help them with? What has been going on in their lives or work that you could perhaps drop them a line on to check their progress? Even a simple 'How are you today?' might serve.

Building, nurturing and leveraging your networking is all about:

- actively promoting others
- engaging and making connection within and across networks
- driving support and sales opportunities for others
- not expecting anything in return
- constantly and consistently adding value to the relationship
- reaching out, asking for help and trusting them to provide you with support.

Be curious about the information you come across and new connections made. How could they help the 12 key people within your network? Have you read, seen or heard something that is worth sharing? What help do those in your network need right now that you can give? What can you do that signals appreciation for the support your key network gives you? Regularly and continuously adding value through communication is integral. Listen to others' dreams and willingly share what you know and who you know to support those dreams.

Only when we network in the right way by choosing, connecting and cultivating our relationships are we able to build networks that matter and that work.

Become known for your value system, integrity and ability to add value. Become known for knowing something. Become known as someone others want to know rather than as someone who continuously takes but doesn't give back.

Your network will fast-track your success, will transform you from the present to your future, will enable you to maximise your impact and drive your influence with those around you.

Download the CULTIVATE worksheet to help you get clear on who you are, what you want and why: **janinegarner.com.au/ resources.**

A gift that keeps on giving

Holly Ransom is the CEO of Emergent, a company that works with global leaders, organisations and governments on the frontiers of change and innovation. In 2012 she was the youngest person to be named in Australia's '100 Most Influential Women', and also became the world's youngest-ever Rotary President (then 22).

Holly attributes much of her success—for example, working with the G20 and the UN—to strategically surrounding herself with the best and brightest leaders, game changers and thought leaders, including Simon Sinek, President Obama and Janine Allis. She knows her power as an influential and valuable change-maker comes from the support team she chooses.

'It takes a village to raise a child, and it takes a whole army to raise a young woman,' Holly jokes when I asked her about the important role her mentors play.

'Growing up as a "different" sort of kid, I relied on my mentors and my beloved grandmother for encouragement and advice, as well as my community in hometown Western Australia for opportunities to connect and learn from others,' she adds.

Holly is a shining example of the transformation that can occur when we surround ourselves with the right people in honest, authentic relationships.

'People are the be-all and end-all for me,' she says. 'My definition of success is that I prioritise quality time with the people I love and care about, and I do everything that I can to support their growth, development and journey too. The notion of relationships being transactional makes me feel ill. I try to

(continued)

159

always make sure my mentors know how grateful I am for the role they play in my life.'

Holly is passionate about ensuring that what she receives, she gives back—but that value also keeps on giving. 'I'm fortunate to have a number of mentees, and I learn an enormous amount from them...and hopefully impart as much back to support them with the challenges and opportunities they're navigating.'

FINAL WORDS

I wrote this book because I am constantly asked, 'Janine, how do I network? How do I find the right people who have the right skills to help me move forward in my life?'

Now you've read this book, the answer to both these questions will be very clear to you.

Get off your butt and do the work.

Reading *It's Who You Know* without putting into action any of the advice or strategies is useless—no, it's crazy!

As you've seen, building a strategic and smart network is the real deal, but you must own the process and commit to investing the time and effort into bringing your network, your personal Nexus of 12 key people, to life.

Everything I have shared in this book I teach and implement myself. When I arrived in Australia in 2000, I had already built a career and a network in the UK, but then I had to start all over again—to find a job, establish my personal brand, build a life and rebuild a career.

In the early days there was no doubt that I was networking to build my profile and business—it was a transactional swapping of business cards and contacts. But as I grew my ideas did too and I experienced firsthand the power of a tight, connected and trusted network of people who work together collaboratively to drive change and momentum for each other.

My network is my solid foundation. I have the right people with me at all times on my journey. Teachers to help stretch my thinking and force me to dig deeper. Promoters to pick me up when I need motivation or to make connections to new opportunities. Butt-kickers keeping me focused and on track. And a steady Pit

Crew, who I could not possibly survive without as a mother, wife, entrepreneur, business owner, philanthropist, dreamer, Connector, health fanatic or friend. I simply would not live a balanced, connected and present life without my 12 key people.

I choose to surround myself with positive, big-picture, can-do thinkers. I choose to surround myself with the right people. This is what fuels the fire in my belly, puts the spring in my step and waters the seeds of ideas that grow in my mind. As my mentor says to me, it's about doing the work I love with the people I love in the way I want to do it.

You are ready now. You are absolutely capable of doing all of this too, of building your very own network of 12 that can help you achieve whatever it is in your personal and professional life that you want to accomplish.

Let the thinking and ideas flow, allow the concept of the 12 key people to sink in, then go back to the relevant chapters in the book and start putting into practice all the things you've learned. Review your network, seek out who you need. Choose to make an impact by developing your own network to connect with the right people in the right way and to cultivate those relationships over the long term.

Remember why you picked up this book in the first place. Maybe you were curious about how to network more effectively, maybe you were feeling disconnected from the world, lacking support or motivation, or maybe you just knew there was a smarter, more successful way to network.

So you've got all the knowledge you need — it's now up to you to use it, to get going. Don't let your network whirl around you at the speed of a tornado. Get in control and build something that works for you.

Networking matters and always will, but it's your network that matters most.

The power is in who you know, and that means surrounding yourself with a small but strong and strategic network — a network that works *with* you and *for* you.

So go on — get off your butt and go and build your network. It's time to find out who you know.

162

ONE LAST CHECKLIST

This is one of the most important checklists in this book.

As we've discussed, the journey you've just undertaken is not a set-and-forget activity, so if you download and print out only one checklist to stick on your wall or in your diary as a reminder, let it be this one.

Your strategic network checklist

Part I: Why

❑ **SHIFT your mindset from disconnection to connection.**

The explosion of social media that has seen a massive increase in our 'connections' has also brought a parallel and related increase in our sense of 'disconnection'.

Social media encourages one-way communication. Sure, we're connected, but increasingly to the digital world rather than to the real world and each other. Effective networking, on the other hand, relies on two-way communication: the mutual exchange of information and value.

The challenge is to build strategic connections around us, assembling a select group of people who open us up to quality thinking and new perspectives.

Building a more valuable network means taking back ownership and control of your network and approaching your actions and connections with strategic deliberation. You have to take ownership of your network and to reassess it continuously so it continues to evolve to meet your changing needs.

❏ **RETHINK how you network — from transactional to transformational.**

Rethinking your network starts with your moving away from transactions, the traditional type of networking, and towards transformations.

Transactional networking does matter; transformational networking, engaging your personal network, matters more. Networking as we know it tends to be shallow, superficial and ineffective. We need to stop trying to be too many things for too many people through merely transacting. Focusing on our core network, we can begin to develop trust along with connected visions and goals, to exchange value to mutual advantage.

For a network that continues to add value, you need to reassess and revise who you know, your goals and how you're going to achieve them. You need people who understand the path you're on, especially when it changes.

To start building any form of effective network you need to make a conscious decision to explore other possibilities and people, then you have to do *something*. It's only through taking action that networking begins to deliver personal value.

❏ **TRANSFORM to a powerful collective network that will fast-track your future success.**

Building a network for personal growth hinges on connecting and collaborating with the right people, openly sharing knowledge and insights with individuals who understand our goals and aspirations, who nurture a collective interest in our own growth and that of the whole group. It is only when we learn to move together that we start to move faster.

The key is to connect with diverse people, because through diversity you build competitive advantage.

At the heart of a successful network lies the concept of value exchange — a mutually beneficial process that relies on more than just a transaction.

To drive your influence, you have to tap into what's around you. Your network must cover key skills. Think of it as your own personal board of advisers, 'intelligence bank', and marketing machine or cheer squad.

Your network will understand your bigger-picture goals and dreams. They will be your sounding board and help shape your thinking. They will help you stay in the zone and develop resilience during the tough times, and will fuel your hunger and belief.

Part II: Who

❏ **SORT through who is in your current network.**

To progress from a transactional network to a strategic and transformational one, you must first assess who is in your network right now. You need to understand your current network before you can change or improve it. This requires some sorting.

The SORT process will help you:

- identify who is in your network right now

- assess the true diversity and integration of your network

- highlight any gaps that may exist.

We commonly gravitate towards the people we spend most time with or have most contact with. We are drawn to clusters of 'sameness', staying in our comfort zone, not pushing ourselves, accepting the status quo.

A strong strategic network relies on diversity, spanning gender, age, experience, culture, industries, organisations and geographical locations, valuing differences of opinion and insight, and out-of-the-box thinking.

SORT is not a one-off, set-and-forget process. Your life and career goals and the people around you change constantly based on where you are in life and at work. So your network must constantly evolve too.

❏ **SEARCH for the Core Four people who must be in your network.**

When creating your strategic network, your first task is to find one key person in each of the four quadrants in your Nexus. Identifying these four personality types should be your starting point when building a network.

The Core Four will include a Promoter (your personal champion and inspiration), a Pit Crew (who keeps you on track and nurtures you), a Teacher (who expands your knowledge and wisdom and pushes you to know more every day), and a Butt-kicker (who holds you accountable for your actions and decisions).

Establishing your Core Four will help ensure you build a network that is balanced and diverse.

Remember, your network isn't static once you have built it. It's a living, breathing thing that will continue to change as you and your needs and goals change.

❏ **SEEK out the 12 key people and personalities for your success now.**

Finding your Core Four is your network's starting point, but real momentum towards your goals kicks in when you expand your Nexus to incorporate 12 key people and personalities.

A quality network of 12 will allow you to build your future strategically, leverage opportunities and mutually exchange value, accelerating you towards inspirational thinking and exponential growth.

Your 12 key people and personalities in the four quadrants are: Cheerleader, Explorer and Inspirer (your Promoters); Lover, Connector and Balancer (Pit Crew); Influencer, Professor and Architect (Teachers); and Truth Sayer, Accelerator and Mentor (Butt-kickers).

You need one person only representing each of the 12 key personality types. This probably means you will need to find people to fill certain roles, but it may also mean reassessing some who are in your network and seeking out other individuals to broaden your network's diversity.

Taking control and strategically aligning yourself with the right people is the best way to fast-track your goals and ambitions.

❏ **SINK any of the 12 Shadow Archetypes who don't add value.**

Building a strategic network is not just about identifying 12 key people; they must be the *right* 12 people. For any kind of success in life, you need to surround yourself with the right crew.

Out of habit or inertia, many of us tolerate personal and professional connections that drain us of energy, inspiration and momentum. Once you identify the negative people in your life who limit your progress, then you can choose how much time, if any, you continue to give them.

Shadow Archetypes who limit your potential and obstruct your goals and success fall into the following four quadrants: Burners (Saboteur, Back-stabber, Dream Stealer) want you to become less; Underminers (Traitor, Narcissist, Energy Vampire) want you to care less; Judgers (Sceptic, Labeller, Villain) want you to know less; and Fighters (Bully, Liar, Critic) want you to do less.

Awareness of the impact others can have on your success brings choice. Knowing who to cut from your network is as important as knowing who to keep. By taking ownership of, and control of the key people in, your network, you can choose to make your network work for you.

Part III: How

❏ **CHOOSE to get clear on who you are and what your goals are.**

To build an effective network you must be clear on what your goals and aspirations are, how others can help you achieve them and how you can help them in return. You need to understand your values, identify your strengths and weaknesses, and above all be authentic and true — to own your vision of you and what it is you want to achieve in your career and life.

What is your area of expertise? Are you owning it? When you are known for knowing something, your ability to cut through the crowd and get noticed increases exponentially.

Getting clarity on the who, what and why of your personal brand will enable you to build a network that works for you. When you embrace your natural style, and work to your strengths, you start to enact change. And when you make life choices that are congruent with your temperament, you unleash vast stores of energy.

You have to be brave, believe in yourself and fear less. It's up to you to get out of your own way, to decide that you want to change what you are doing right now, to take control of your network and to drive your future success.

❏ **CONNECT with the right people in the right way.**

To network successfully you must ensure you are constantly surrounded by people who will stretch you, challenge your thinking and hold you accountable for your decisions.

Think strategically about who you want to connect with and look around you for anyone who might help make an introduction. Be clear on who and what you need, be curious and explore what's out there, and make a decision based on what works and what doesn't work for you.

Be willing to step out of your comfort zone. Dig deep and move beyond the place of familiarity and safety to connect with people outside your traditional circle. Remember, this is your journey and your network.

Connection is not simply about hitting the 'let's connect' button. You have to engage fully, share value, take the lead, be an example to others in your network, model the behaviour you seek in return.

Investing the time to review your network regularly is essential. Nurturing a transformational network is an ongoing process. It is not something you switch on when you want something and switch off when it's not needed.

❑ **CULTIVATE those relationships and mutually exchange value, sharing insight and information that matters to them.**

Networking is a shared experience. When you network with conviction, sure of who you are and what you know, willingly sharing information and insights that matter to others, you create opportunities, exchange value and increase your influence. Connections become transformational.

There are 10 secrets to cultivating your connections for successful networking:

- First impressions count.
- Confidence matters.
- Speak up to be heard.
- Listen to be present.
- Become an action taker.
- Exchange value.
- Identify yourself.
- Be memorable.
- Follow your energy.
- Keep your network alive.

Become known for your value system, integrity and ability to add value. Build a reputation as someone others want to know rather than as someone who continuously takes but doesn't give back.

Your network will fast-track your success, transform you from the present to your future, maximise your impact and drive your influence with those around you.

A small, strategic and supercharged network relies on collaboration and connection. But most of all, the process must be fun! Don't forget to enjoy the ride and the journey as the magic happens. I guarantee this will transform not just your network, but *your life*.

NOTES

1. Hanna Krasnova et al. (2013), 'Envy on Facebook: A Hidden Threat to Users' Life Satisfaction?', AISeL.

2. Annual report, 2015–2016, World Economic Forum.

3. Multiple sources, e.g. Forbes.com, 18 July 2012.

4. Mikael Strandberg, '9 Tips to Becoming a Modern Day Explorer', *Huffington Post*, 1 October 2013.

5. *Personality and Individual Differences* 52 (1), January 2012, 56–60, ScienceDirect.

6. Jennifer Merrill, *Chronicle of Evidence-Based Mentoring*, 7 November 2016.

7. 'The UPS Store Makes "Mentoring Month" Matter for Small Business Owners', 9 January 2014.

8. Laura Entis, '5 Famous Business Leaders on the Power of Mentorship', *Entrepreneur*, 6 August 2015.

9. Madeline Stone, '9 of the most inspiring rags-to-riches stories in business', *Business Insider*, 25 October 2015.

10. Ellen Cobb, 'Workplace bullying: a global overview', *Management Issues*, 8 July 2011.

INDEX

Accelerator (Butt-kicker) 73, 94–96

accountability 55, 64–65, 66, 92, 95, 96, 133, 140, 166, 168

Amazon 122

Apple 122

Architect (Teacher) 73, 90–92

assessing current network 11, 13–15, 42, 45–49, 99; *see also* diversity
— balanced 50–51
— closed vs open 49–50
— gender make-up 45–46
— identify members 42, 43–44
— location of members 45, 47–49
— similarities among members 45, 46–47

authenticity 10, 11, 92, 119, 128, 147, 159, 168

avoidance of networking 1, 6–8, 17
— pain points 6–8

Back-stabber (Burner) 104, 105, 106–107

balanced and integrated network 50–51

Balancer (Pit Crew) 72, 73, 84–85

Beatles 121

Become an action taker (10 secrets) 145, 151–152

Be memorable (10 secrets) 146, 155–156

benefits of networking 1–37, 163

Bezos, Jeff 122

board of advisers 33–34, 35

Bono 122

Browne, Melissa 51–52

building network 115–159

Bully (Fighters) 105, 111

Burners (Shadow Archetype) 104, 105, 106–107, 113
— Back-stabber 104, 105, 106–107
— Dream Stealer 104, 105, 107
— Saboteur 104, 105, 106

Butt-kicker (Core Four) 55, 56, 64–66, 73, 92–98, 115, 161; *see also* Core Four
— Accelerator 73, 94–96
— Mentor 73, 96–98
— Truth Sayer 73, 92–94

case studies 12, 25, 36–37,
129, 136, 141
challenging and stretching
functions 20, 21, 34, 37, 62,
93, 115, 129, 133, 168
changing your network
133–134
Cheerleader (Promoter) 72, 73,
74–75
choice 7, 113–114
clarity on goals and identity
117–129, 167–168
coffee roulette 137
collaboration 28, 29
—vs competition 27, 31–33
collective network 27–37
comfort zone 17, 25, 36, 37,
47, 59, 64, 102, 123, 127,
137, 165, 168
communication 157–158
—one-way 5–6, 163
—skills 10–11
—two-way 6
competition vs collaboration
27, 31–33
confidence 120, 148, 168
Confidence matters (10 secrets)
145, 147–148
congruence with natural style
126–127
connect and connection(s) 1, 3,
82–83, 116, 117, 131–141
—building 28, 29
—choosing 117–129
—cultivating 116, 117–129,
131, 141, 143–160, 169
—Link in 134, 138–130
—LinkedIn 138–139, 152

—right people 118–119,
131–141, 168–169
—right way 1, 2, 116, 117,
131–160, 169
—three actions for
134–139
—ten secrets of cultivating
145–160, 169
—vs disconnecting 4–6
Connector (Pit Crew) 72, 73,
82–83
Contactually (software) 23
control of network 11–12, 37,
113–114
Core Four 52, 118, 129; see
also twelve key people
—characteristics and roles
54–60
—examples 56
—filling gaps 68–69,
115–159
—four elements 53–56
—four roles 53
—four key characters
53–54
—Hogwarts Houses 54, 56
—identify 12 people 71–99
—identify your 53–69
—purpose of 115, 161–162
—Role 1 Promoter 55,
56–58, 72, 73, 74–79,
115, 161
—Role 2 Pit Crew 55, 56,
59–61, 72, 73, 79–86,
115, 161
—Role 3 Teacher 55, 56,
62–63, 73, 86–92,
115, 161

—Role 4 Butt-kicker 55, 56, 64–66, 73, 92–98, 115, 161
—search for 40, 52, 53–69, 71, 166
—starting point for network 54–60
Critic (Fighters) 105, 112
cultivate connections 116, 117–129, 131, 141, 143–160; *see also* connect and connection(s)
—relationships and exchange value 143–160, 169
—ten secrets 145–160, 169
current practice 14–15
cutting people from network *see* negative people

dabbling 15, 17
deliver on promises 151–152
depth of network 23–24
differentiation 155
Disconnect (movie) 3–4
diversity and diversification 10, 20, 21, 29–30, 41, 42, 45–46, 49–52, 164
Dream Stealer (Burner) 104, 105, 107

effective networking 15, 18–19, 21–23; *see also* exponential networking; transaction/transactional networking; transactional to transformational networking; transforming your network
Emergent 159–160

Energy Vampire (Underminer) 105, 109
engagement 10, 22, 35, 128–139
events 4, 6, 7, 136–137
example, setting an 140–141
exchange value 30–31, 32–33, 34, 117, 118, 131, 143, 136, 140–141, 144–145, 158, 164
—cultivating connections 116, 117–129, 131, 141, 143–160, 169
Exchange value (10 secrets) 146, 153–154
expertise and skills 119, 121–123
Explorer (Promoter) 72, 73, 76–77
exponential networking 15, 19–23, 27–37, 41
extroversion vs introversion *see* introversion vs extroversion

fear 5, 16, 17, 59, 93, 95, 109, 118, 168
—reducing 127–128
Fighters (Shadow Archetype) 105, 110–112, 113
—Bully 105, 111
—Critic 105, 112
—Liar 105, 111
First impressions count (10 secrets)141, 145, 146–147
Flemming, Alison 140
focus, benefits of 35–36
Fogden-Moore, Nikki 85

follow-up 4, 139–140, 151–152
Follow your energy (10 secrets) 146, 156–157
FOMO (Fear of Missing Out) 5, 124
Four Core people *see* Core Four

gaps, filling 115–160
garbage in, garbage out 155–156
Gates, Bill 123, 125
gender make-up of network 45–46
givers vs takers 30–31
giving back *see also* sharing; value exchange
—value of 30–31, 160
—vs taking 19
Gladwell, Malcolm 121, 146
goals and aspirations 19, 52, 78, 83, 95, 115, 120, 125, 129
—clarity on your 117–129, 167–169
—identifying your 116, 118–119, 165, 167
—owning your 119–121
grit 60
groupthink 50
growth, personal 1, 6, 11, 22, 23, 28, 29, 33, 41, 51, 62, 72, 74, 91, 97, 103, 109, 123, 128, 159, 164

Hang out to connect 134, 136–138
Hogwarts Houses 54, 56
Hoitink, Suzie 36–37

Holzherr, Nick 76–77, 141
how of networking 115–160, 167–169
—choose clarity on goals and identity 117–129, 167–168
—connect with right people in the right way 131–141, 168–169
—cultivate relationships and exchange value 116, 117–129, 131, 141, 143–160, 169
Hunger Games, The 27–28

Identify yourself (10 secrets) 146, 154
identity, your 124–126, 167–168
—clarity on 117–129, 167–168
ineffective networking 14, 15, 16–17; *see also* effective networking
Influencer (Teacher) 73, 86–88
ingredients of a powerful network 33–35
—board of advisers 33–34, 35
—intelligence bank 33, 34, 35
Inspirer (Promoter) 72, 73, 78–79
integrity 25, 92, 93, 111, 151, 158, 169
intelligence bank 33, 34, 35
introversion vs extroversion 123–126, 156–157
isolation 5–6

job clinging 16–17
Jolie, Angelina 122
Judgers (Shadow Archetype) 105, 109–110, 113
— Sceptic 105, 109
— Labeller 105, 110
— Villain 105, 110

Keep your network (10 secrets) alive 146, 157–158
key people *see* twelve key people

Labeller (Judger) 105, 110
Law of Reciprocity 31
learning 62–63, 88–89
Liar (Fighters) 105, 111
like-minded people 49–50
LinkedIn 138–139, 152
Link in to connect 134, 138–130
Listen to be present (10 secrets) 145, 150–151
loneliness 5–6
Lover (Pit Crew) 72, 73, 80–81

McAdams, Lisa 25
maintaining your network 146, 151–152, 157–158, 168–169
managing your network 151–152
marketing machine 33, 35
'Matchers' 31; *see also* givers vs takers
members of network 39–114; *see also* Core Four; twelve key people

Mentor (Butt-kicker) 73, 96–98
mentors and mentoring 135–136, 137, 159–160
mindset, shift 3–12, 163

Narcissist (Underminer) 105, 108
negative people, removing 40, 101–114, 116, 129, 167
— Burners (Shadow Archetype) 104, 105, 106–107, 113
— Fighters (Shadow Archetype) 105, 110–112, 113
— Judgers (Shadow Archetype) 105, 109–110, 113
— Underminers (Shadow Archetype) 105, 107–109, 113
networking down 136
Nexus of Core Four *see* Core Four

opportunities, creating 117, 131, 143, 145
ownership
— goals 119–121
— self 119–121, 124–126
— what you are doing 121–123
— your network 11–12, 22, 28, 113–114, 163
pain points in networking 6–8
paralysis by analysis 64
passions 119, 157
passivity 16–17, 18

personalities, Four Core 40,
    54–55, 67, 69, 71–99, 103,
    115, 120, 154, 166–167; see
    also Core Four
personality, your 116, 117–129,
    136
    —identifying your 117–129,
    147–148
    —congruence 126–127
Pit Crew (Core Four) 55, 56,
    59–61, 72, 73, 79–86
    —Lover 72, 73, 80–81
    —Connector 72, 73, 82–83
    —Balancer 72, 73, 84–85
Poduri, Chax 12
power pose 148
present, being 7–8, 10, 139,
    141, 147
procrastination 15, 17, 24, 65,
    95, 96, 126
Professor (Teacher) 73, 88–90
Promoter (Core Four) 55, 56–
    58, 72, 73, 74–79
    —Cheerleader 72, 73,
    74–75
    —Explorer 72, 73, 76–77
    —Inspirer 72, 73, 78–79

Ransom, Holly 159–160
Reach out to connect
    134–136
reasons for networking 1–37
relationships, cultivating
    143–159
respecting others' time
    139–140, 141
rethinking your network
    13–25, 164; see also diversity

reviewing your network
    168–169
reworking your network 10–11
right way to network 2, 13–25
    —key stages in 1–37
ripple effect 46

Saboteur (Burner) 104, 105, 106
Scentre Group 140
Sceptic (Judger) 105, 109
self-belief see confidence
self-promotion 128
six degrees of separation
    134–135
Shadow Archetypes, removing
    from network 101–114, 116,
    129, 167
sharing 33, 121–122, 140,
    153–154, 169; see also
    exchange value
shifting attitude to networking,
    importance of 2, 3–12
Sivan, Troye 35
size of network 23–24, 33, 52;
    see also Core Four; twelve
    key people
social media 5, 50
    —isolation 5–6
    —one-way communication
    5–6, 163
sort current network 40,
    41–52, 165–166
    —two phases 42–49
    —worksheet for 44
Speak up to be heard (10
    secrets) 145, 148–150
stages in building a network,
    four 39–114

—1 sort, establishing current 40, 41–52
—2 search for core four 40, 59–69
—3 seek 12 key people 40, 71–99
—4 remove negative people 40, 101–114
stages of networking, three 15–21; *see also* effective networking; exponential networking; ineffective networking; transaction/transactional networking; transactional to transformational networking; transforming your network
strategic network, checklist for 163–169
—how 167–169
—who 165–167
—why 163–165
strengths, your 29, 34, 97, 118, 119, 120, 122, 125–126, 128, 138, 167–168
success 86–87, 132, 148

takers vs givers 30–31
Teacher (Core Four) 55, 56, 62–63, 86–92
—Architect 73, 90–92
—Influencer 73, 86–88
—Professor 73, 88–90
ten secrets of cultivating connections 145–160, 169
—1 First impressions count 145, 146–147
—2 Confidence matters 145, 147–148

—3 Speak up to be heard 145, 148–150
—4 Listen to be present 145, 150–151
—5 Become an action taker 145, 151–152
—6 Exchange value 146, 153–154
—7 Identify yourself 146, 154
—8 Be memorable 146, 155–156
—9 Follow your energy 146, 156–157
—10 Keep your network alive 146, 157–158
thanks, offering 151–152
Traitor (Underminer) 105, 108
transact/transactional networking 1, 15, 21–23, 132, 136, 138–139, 159–160, 161, 165
transactional to transformational networking 15, 19, 21–23, 42, 164
transforming your network 2, 15, 20–23, 24, 27–37, 40, 41–42, 127, 132, 134, 138–139, 145, 152, 159–160, 164–165, 168–169; *see also* stages of networking transform
twelve key people, 133, 151
—Core Four 1: Promoter 55, 56–58, 72, 73, 74–79, 115, 161; Cheerleader 72, 73, 74–75; Explorer 72, 73, 76–77; Inspirer 72, 73, 78–79

twelve key people (*Cont'd*)
— Core Four 2: Pit Crew 55,
   56, 59–61, 72, 73, 79–86,
   161–162; Lover 72, 73,
   80–81; Connector 72, 73,
   82–83; Balancer 72, 73,
   84–85
— Core Four 3: Teacher 55,
   56, 62–63, 86–92, 115,
   161; Influencer 73, 86–
   88; Professor 73, 88–90;
   Architect 73, 90–92
— Core Four 4: Butt-kicker
   55, 56, 64–66, 92–98,
   115, 161; Accelerator 73,
   94–96; Mentor 73, 96–98;
   Truth Sayer 73, 92–94
— filling gaps 115–160
— power of 144–145
— search for 40, 71–99,
   166–167
Truth Sayer (Butt-kicker) 73,
   92–94

Underminers (Shadow
   Archetype) 105, 107–109,
   113
— Energy Vampire 105, 109
— Narcissist 105, 108
— Traitor 105, 108

value, add 14, 30, 43, 114, 141,
   149, 157, 158, 164, 169
value exchange *see* exchange
   value
values, your 93, 119, 121, 123,
   158, 167, 169
Villain (Judger) 105, 110

vision, your 119, 120, 127
Voice, The 147

weaknesses, your 29, 32, 118,
   119, 120, 167–168
web of you 140–141
where to start 39–40
Whisk.com 141
who of networking 39–114,
   165–167; *see also* Core Four;
   negative people, removing;
   twelve key people
— sort current network 41–
   52, 165–166
— Core Four, search for
   53–69, 166
— Shadow Archetypes,
   removing 40, 101–114,
   167
— twelve key people, search
   for 71–99, 166–167
who you need in your network;
   see also assessing current
   network; Core Four; twelve
   key people
why, your 126–127
why of networking 1–37,
   163–165
— rethink network 13–35,
   164
— shift mindset 3–12, 163
— transform your network
   27–37, 164–165
Wizard of Oz, The 118
World Economic Forum 29

LET'S CONNECT

This is a book about networking and authentic connection, so naturally it's fitting that you and I should connect!

But don't just fall back into transactional networking, I'd love for you to reach out and tell me what you learned and applied from this book. Has it helped you get a new job, accelerate your business growth or achieve a personal goal? Do you feel more supported and connected?

My regular blog posts are a great way of keeping in touch and inspired on whatever journey you are on. Help is at hand in other forms as well. For the gals, you might like to check out my smart and supercharged networking community LBDGroup. For everyone, I regularly speak, consult and coach on collaboration, networking and real leadership — it's all about keeping you connected and creative.

Reading this book is your first foray into transforming your network. The real power now lies in your hands.

Just remember that this really is a journey. It's a journey to *who you know*. And I'd love to know more about you.

Janine

janinegarner.com.au
@janinegarner
info@janinegarner.com.au

LBD Group
thelbdgroup.com.au
@LBDGroup